THE HOUSE OF DR KOOLHAAS

THE HOUSE OF DR KOOLHAAS

FRANÇOISE FROMONOT

A GUMSHOE BOOK

PARK BOOKS

'When I don't know what to do, I start looking at things. There's a technique for this, too, or rather many techniques. I have my own, which consists in working backward from a series of images to a state of affairs.'
—Michelangelo Antonioni,
That Bowling Alley on the Tiber, 1976[1]

'Dreams are no longer summoned with closed eyes, but in reading; and a true image is now a product of learning: it derives from words spoken in the past, exact recensions, the amassing of minute facts, monuments reduced to infinitesimal fragments, and the reproductions of reproductions. In the modern experience these elements contain the power of the impossible... The imaginary is not formed in opposition to reality as its denial or compensation; it grows among signs, from book to book, in the interstice of repetitions and commentaries; it is born and takes shape in the interval between books. It is a phenomenon of the library.'
—Michel Foucault, 'Fantasia of the Library', 1967[2]

Madelon Vriesendorp & OMA, Villa dall'Ava, Saint-Cloud, View B, 1987

PROLOGUE

Bastille Day 2009. As they do every year, the Bs are hosting a little garden party at their Saint-Cloud home. The garden is calm and fresh, the house delightful. At the end of the evening the hosts will usher us to the roof terrace to admire the fireworks over the Eiffel Tower. But for the moment it is still light. Most of the guests are already here: friends of the Bs, family, a few architects. The couple show their visitors around the place – she, in an elegant black dress that sets off her piercing eyes; he, in a white shirt and heavy-framed glasses, waxing lyrical when talk turns to 'the villa'. Both speak of how enchanting it is to live in this little haven overlooking Paris, their home now for almost 20 years.

As day blurs into dusk, the rooftop swimming pool lights up, a trench of aquamarine. The Airparif balloon floats in the distance like a full moon, a milky globe suspended in the dying light. Standing on the deck, we try to make out the skyscrapers of La Défense – and to resist the pull of the void that beckons from behind the soft mesh fencing. Down below, a vaguely familiar silhouette flits across the garden, her hair pale gold, her summer dress sea-green. A round of introductions. Everyone babbles their name – what do you say to an apparition? She's used to it by now. 'Catherine', she says, extending her hand.

The Bs take her on a tour of the property in the company of a young French OMA associate. He is handsome, very enthusiastic; he blushes a lot. She looks around. The pick-up sticks at the entrance, the twisting stairs in the hall, the translucent apron around the kitchen, the pipework spilling like entrails over the shower wall, the oculus at the foot of the swimming pool – her presence seems suddenly to bring out all the strangeness, the irony of the place. *Belle de jour, belle de nuit*. The tour pauses in the Bs' bedroom, in front of the striped ply that covers a partition wall: 'There wasn't much money left over for the interior. Which gave us the chance to experiment', the young architect explains, his cheeks ablaze. She sketches a dreamy smile.

Like in a theatre foyer during the intermission, the guests have spread out between the buffet in the garden and the glow of the living room. The conversation rambles. 'You know', she says out of the blue, through the smoke of her nth cigarette, 'Marcello would have liked to have been an architect'. More than her face or her celebrated blondeness, it is her voice – her delivery, a little rushed and monotone – that calls up a flood of images: so many characters, so many stories. Her every utterance colours the air with memories that make the evening and its setting even more unreal.

At nightfall, we all gather near the swimming pool for the party's final spectacle. For some reason – the distance from Paris, perhaps, or the breeze that has risen to the west, or a technical malfunction – we do not hear the explosion of fireworks that erupts from the Champ de Mars. Above the city plunged into darkness, the Eiffel Tower ignites noiselessly, as in a silent film.

THE VILLA OF MYSTERIES

If the interest of a building derives from its capacity to surprise – to make you more confused the more you look at it, to play on your expectations only to overturn what you thought you already knew – then the Villa dall'Ava must be one of the most intriguing examples of late-twentieth-century architecture. Each of us can picture its capsized volumes, its eccentric claddings and its aerial swimming pool, pointed like a dart at the Eiffel Tower. But despite the fame of its designer, whose every act or gesture, however slight, has been systematically dissected for decades, the villa itself remains somewhat

Rooftop pool, Villa dall'Ava

Elevated view of front facade

apart from the rest of his work, like a little folly shielded by the paradoxes that it seems to cultivate at will. At once extrovert and sibylline, spectacular but difficult to capture on film, it can barely be seen from the street and is not open to the public. Ultimately, we know only two or three things about it, and these facts are endlessly rehashed like the official biography of a star with a ubiquitous screen persona but closely guarded private life. The villa was commissioned in 1984 from Rem Koolhaas and his Office for Metropolitan Architecture by and for Dominique and Lydie Boudet and their daughter. (Monsieur works as an economics journalist for a large construction media group. Madame, *née* dall'Ava, is a psychologist.) It was completed only in 1991, following a lengthy stoppage when the neighbours brought a lawsuit against the long, glazed facade that was to border their property. On the upper floor are two mini-apartments

Rem Koolhaas at the Villa dall'Ava, 1991

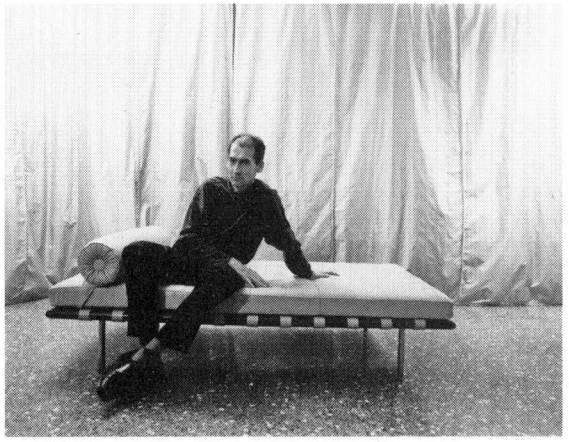

contained in two boxes – the parents' one looks onto the garden, mademoiselle's the street. Below the apartments is a narrow glass box housing the shared spaces – living room, kitchen – above them, the rooftop swimming pool. This layered confection is placed on a concrete base that is wedged into the slope and clad in *opus incertum*; the base contains the service spaces and M Boudet's office. In the interior, these three levels and their heterogeneous volumes are connected by a circuit of stairs supplemented, between the entrance and the living room, by a ramp.

How, then, to relate the analytical clarity of this spatial organisation to the evident confusion that its architecture provokes? The moment the villa was completed, critics and historians competed to put their bafflement

Front gate

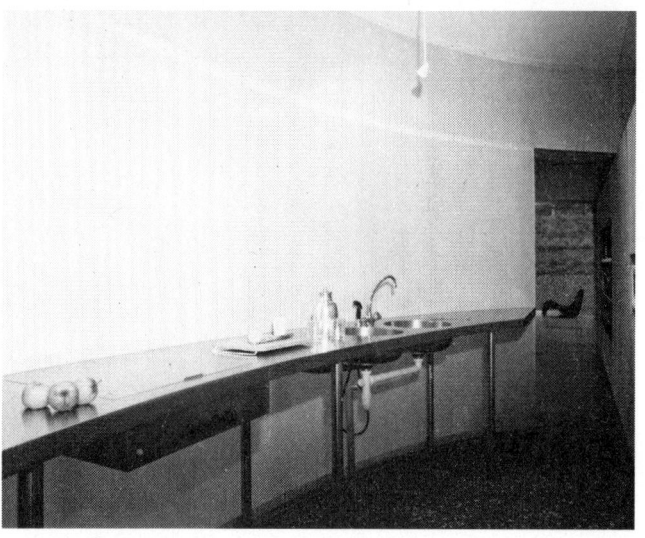

Curving kitchen wall

Looking up towards the living room

into words, summoning a host of oxymorons: a 'metropolitan villa' (Bernard Leupen and Christoph Grafe), a 'built manifesto: a social condenser for the family' (Bart Lootsma), a 'microcosm 'enlarged' to its near and far limits' (Jacques Lucan), a 'suburban subversion' of the Parisian *hôtel particulier* (Jean-Louis Cohen).[3] Others appreciated the bravura provocation of this 'splendid prototype of a modernity out of balance' (François Chaslin), this 'fierce and exultant cry in the face of our times' (Jean-Paul Robert).[4] The villa was also the subject of an educational documentary for the ARTE television channel, in which an elaborate soundtrack and scenes in accelerated motion add a touch of incongruity that contrasts with the analytical calm of the voice-over (Richard Copans).[5] Such is the fictional potency of this little house that it even inspired a short epistolary novel, through which it flits as the pretext and backdrop to a narrative of elusive moods (Christophe Van Gerrewey).[6]

And yet, far from exhausting interpretation, the analyses and commentaries that have taken the villa as their subject have had the opposite effect of deepening its mysteries, adding to its singular appeal. 'I do not mean that Connoisseurs and lovers of art find no words with which to praise such objects to us', Sigmund Freud wrote in this regard: 'They are eloquent enough, it seems to me. But usually in the presence of a great work of art each says something different from the other; and none of them says anything that solves the enigma for the unpretending admirer. In my opinion, what grasps us so powerfully can only be the artist's *intention*, in

---

Staircase up to the terrace and pool

so far as he has succeeded in expressing it in his work and in getting us to understand it.'[7] What, then, was Rem Koolhaas trying to achieve with the Villa dall'Ava, this little house that is so captivating and so bizarre, at this precise moment in his thinking and his career? What theoretical project was he devising for it – and through it? If one of the great pleasures of criticism is to take up the challenge posed by such a project, to use the curiosity it provokes as the means to try to decipher its intrigue (at the risk of getting lost in the byways of supposition) before finally attempting to construct, as an 'unpretending admirer', a few hypotheses regarding its author's motives, then the Villa dall'Ava remains an undeniably great and inexhaustible critical subject.

All the more so as its mysteries are not confined to its appearance. To start with, it was the first – and for a long time the only – building Rem Koolhaas realised in the Paris region.[8] The Dutch architect has always been drawn to the French capital, and the projects he has invented in his efforts to seduce her are among his most extraordinary works. However, between the international competition for the Parc de la Villette in 1982 and the consultations on Les Halles and La Défense in the 2000s, OMA has suffered nothing but disappointment in Paris. And yet (another paradox), far from remaining a dead letter, each of these failures has left behind spoils that have become relics of sorts: the striped lung of La Villette, the chessboard of Nanterre, the box of ribbons at Jussieu, the gruyère of the Très Grande Bibliothèque, the seismograph of Les Halles. These rejected proposals have been, and still are, more debated, admired and influential –

Internal staircases

in short, more alive – than those of the pretenders who prevailed over them in their day. Although Paris and the architect courted each other for three decades, their relationship remained platonic, with one single exception – this villa perched in the heights of Saint-Cloud, the precious fruit of a one-night stand.

By a further irony, this little house is one of the first works that Koolhaas built after the publication of *Delirious New York*, the book that established him as the theoretician of the modern metropolis.[9] More exactly, the Villa dall'Ava is situated between that 'retroactive manifesto for Manhattan' and the doctrinal texts on the city in the age of globalisation that Koolhaas would write in the early 1990s and publish in his next book, *S,M,L,XL*.[10] In step with other OMA projects of the same period, each of these texts proclaims in its own way the primacy of urbanism over architecture, whether this is through 'Bigness', a trenchant meditation on the mutation of the discipline unleashed by the invention of very large structures, or 'Whatever Happened to Urbanism?', an impassioned plea for an 'urbanism of uncertainty' that would supplant architecture and its limitations, or 'The Generic City', a gritty portrait of the emerging urban condition shaped by globalisation and hypermodernity. A tale of the twentieth-century invention of 'metropolitan congestion' illustrated with a small house for the enlightened bourgeoisie of the capital of the nineteenth century: inevitably, this brings to mind the most flamboyant antecedent of this apparent paradox – Le Corbusier, also the author, in the

---

S,M,L,XL, 010 Publishers, 1995

1920s, of villas on the doorstep of a Paris that he yearned to align with his diagnosis of a rapidly changing world.

To complicate matters further, Koolhaas seems to enjoy defusing the unease that he triggers, doubling down on his pre-emptive denials of the inexplicable nature of the villa: to listen to him, the project is quite simply the product of a logical, rational – even overly rational – resolution of the conflicting constraints of the site and the programme. The description of the villa on the OMA website is a collage of seemingly objective assertions that, pieced together, make for an argument so patchy it seems fabricated to let us see the holes. These gaps, these things left unsaid, become so many subtexts lurking between the lines, ultimately raising more questions than they answer. Whether out of natural reserve, a taste for concision, a dislike for sharing confidences, or a slight perversity, Koolhaas has always declined to comment on his projects. As if dealing with a simpleton asking for a joke to be explained, he responds to questions on this subject with a stubborn refusal to elaborate, not unreasonably pointing out that this is the role of the critic.[11]

The starting point of the following enquiry is simple, perhaps naïve and most certainly paranoiac. Beyond (or percolating below) Koolhaas's theoretical texts – which he is not so parsimonious with – his orchestration of words and images offers many clues to his work as an architect. If, individually, one is as tortuous as the other, then bringing them together (in some kind of convergence, collision, confrontation, or just by chance) may shed some light on them both. The Villa dall'Ava is a privileged witness to the culture and thinking of the architect at a critical moment in his career. And since it seems to set up a game-like or dreamlike chain of enigmas, then why not try to consider it based on what the architect shows of it, or rather on what he tells us while exposing it to view?

For this, let's return to the book in which Koolhaas presents the villa in detail, his famous monumental monograph *S,M,L,XL*. Just like Le Corbusier with his *Oeuvre complète*, Koolhaas conceived this publication as a work on his work, an architecture project in itself, size XS.[12] Compressed between its metallic boards are 20 years of OMA production as reformulated by the architect himself – all the better to pique curiosity. The blurb on the back cover places the book in the dual category of fiction and vision: this is 'a novel about architecture' that proclaims itself a 'free fall in the space of the typographic imagination', an 'accumulation of words and images that illuminates the condition of architecture today' – all the better to feed speculation. The order of appearance of the works eschews the usual arrangements of this type of publication, with its expected registers (chronology, information, justification), in favour of a structure more conducive to the chance encounters (objective or not) of undirected exploration – all the better to stimulate the imagination. Besides the approach to grouping the projects, which are ranged along with their associated texts in increasing size like clothes along a rail, a single connecting thread weaves through the book: a glossary that runs down the left-hand margin, sometimes breaking off for no apparent reason and then picking up again just as abruptly. The words surreptitiously contaminate the adjoining images with their meanings, an effect redoubled, deflected, or defused by the quotations chosen to illustrate them – enough to inspire free association. The list of sources for the quotes at the end of the book offers what is undoubtedly a very calculated overview of the library of the architect – all the better to speculate on his culture. In order to give a fresh cast to projects that had been seen and reviewed a hundred times before, the visual space developed by Koolhaas with the graphic designer Bruce Mau builds up a profusion of iconography within a structure of independent 'events'; readers can move between these episodes at will, drifting from one to the next, composing their own visual and literary psychogeography according to their research or their mood. These sequences are peppered with textual and visual interruptions, inserts and inlays that are sunk like mines into the flesh of the volume – all the better to encourage exegesis. To paraphrase Koolhaas in his memorable introduction to *Delirious New York*, *S,M,L,XL* is a mountain of evidence clearly assembled to trigger interpretation.[13]

FREEZE-FRAMES

The sequence devoted to the Villa dall'Ava appears in the S section, between the renovation of a hotel in the Swiss Alps and a bus stop in Groningen. Koolhaas evidently attaches great importance to this small building, since it takes up 64 pages, or 32 spreads. At first glance, the ingredients borrow from the standard repertoire of the monograph: texts, images and plans. But Koolhaas only invokes these conventions in order to subvert them, to load them with anomalies seemingly designed to sow doubt and confusion. The opening spread appears to fulfil the liminal role of the site plan. Except that it reproduces, at a scale at which the villa is invisible, a satellite image of a Paris rendered unrecognisable by its reduction to its southwest quarter. However, this displacement towards Saint-Cloud does not put the building at the centre of the picture: on the contrary, the thick black circle that marks its location is exiled to the very edge of the photograph, sliced in two by the glossary that runs down the margin. On the other hand, this arrangement sets up a symmetrical relation between the Eiffel Tower on one side of the centrefold and the villa on the other. In the absence of a title, we may note that the longest entry in the accompanying glossary is headed 'Cities'. The villa could thus be seen as a metonym: despite its scale, it takes as its subject the metropolis – a Paris symbolised by the monumental banner of its modern splendour, which it engages in a private dialogue.

OMA, axonometric silhouette, Villa dall'Ava, 1985

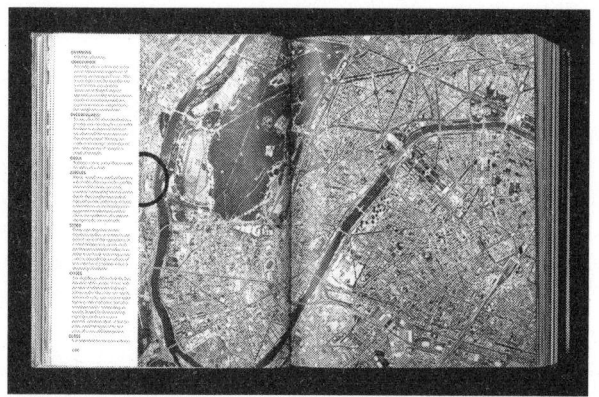
Opening Villa dall'Ava spread from S,M,L,XL, 1995

The villa makes its entrance on the following spread, this time pictured from a bird's-eye view. Yet still we do not *see* it: its volume has been cut out and assimilated into a white surface that simultaneously delineates and obliterates it. Koolhaas seems purposely to delay its unveiling, to make us wait for – and thus desire – the moment of its inauguration. Is the intention to relate its silhouette to the constraints imposed by planning regulations and the shape of the plot (two arguments he invariably invokes to explain its special appearance)? This seems unlikely, as the image in no way explains the villa's context and even serves to accentuate the contrast with its surroundings. Flattened under this inverse *poché*, white on black, as if cloaked in tarpaulin – in short, hidden by the thing that designates it – the villa floats like a spectre among the other houses.

And its appearance is postponed still further. For facing this abstract and vaguely baleful form, Koolhaas places the third canonical element of any monograph,

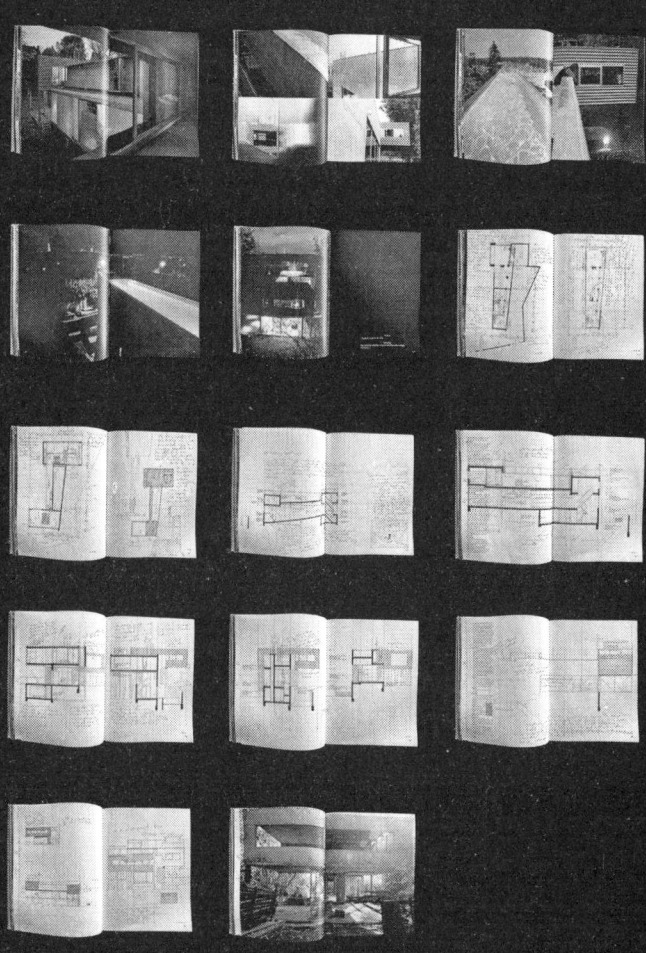

Villa dall'Ava page spreads from S,M,L,XL, 1995

Pilotis and elevated front bedroom

the text of the architect. But instead of the expected explanation or theoretical justification, he delivers a brief history of the 'Obstacles' to the project that reads like the screenplay for some kind of retrospective fable. Its very short episodes, each one matched with a title, are also printed white on black like the title cards of a silent film. The tone of the narrative echoes various film genres, from thrillers to slapstick – an impression reinforced by entries like 'Classic' and 'Clichés' in the lexicon that continues to nod and wink at us from the side of the page. From the origin of the commission, the pretext for a *film noir*-style opening ('Letter. It was handwritten in blue ink, obviously by someone who was very passionate about architecture... It had a desperate tone: 'you are our last chance') to its paradoxical denouement ('They moved in because it was still not finished... We became friends'), Koolhaas sketches in successive strokes a parable of the condition of the architect that is reminiscent of many of his reflections on the subject: 'Only the relentless highlighting of the horrifying conditions that have spawned contemporary architecture – and which could easily assume the dimensions of a Greek tragedy – can reveal the paradoxical fact that to be an architect today is, regardless of individual worth, to be a hero', as he has written elsewhere.[14]

This tragi-comic scenario of long-past events is followed by a pictorial tour of the completed villa. The unfolding of this sequence, the way it introduces the characters and then takes us on a walk around and inside the villa, adds to the feeling that we're being shown the storyboard of a plot in which the villa is both the protagonist and the stage. Still seen from above, but now unveiled, it glows, fiery and fragile amongst the heavy-set houses of this opulent residential suburb, which are shown faded to a dull bister in an apparent reproach to their age, their conventionality, their ordinariness. Then the camera touches down in the street and we see the villa, all made up with lighting, emerge over the boundary wall. A fire seems to be consuming it from within: the incandescent mask of its facade leers through two half-open windows at the street below. The familiar, reassuring picture of domestic life has become a disturbing phantasmagoria.

All the images that follow seem equally intent on throwing us off our bearings, on increasing our unease. Destabilisation of gravity: frontal views accentuate the imbalance of the object they frame. In the garden facade, for example, the volume of the Bs' apartment rests on the fragile glass box of the living room, which is itself displaced towards the post that constitutes its sole identifiable support. Voyeurism: a young woman appears in the light of an upstairs window, a sleeping body can be made out in a reflection. Illusion: the artificial lighting paints the spaces in unreal colours, accentuates the kitsch materials, and reveals, through reverberation, recesses that are otherwise hidden. Personification of the inanimate: chairs and stairs are transformed into sculptural figures, into *characters*; objects are used to simulate genre scenes; a Le Corbusier LC1 Basculant chair at the head of a Mies Barcelona daybed mimics a psychoanalysis session against a backdrop of white curtains, drawn like a cyclorama. Mixing of scales, implausible details, humour: a giraffe held on a leash by an attendant moves along the driveway, its progress visible through the glass facade of the interior ramp. In this madhouse, the pet is bigger than his master.

And then there are the incomprehensible iconographic imports, red herrings, enigmas within the enigma, that surface along the way. A black-and-white press photograph of a screaming trader at the Paris Bourse suddenly turns up in a double-page spread. A Vermeer painting (*A Young Woman Seated at a Virginal*, c 1670) is embedded into a view of the side facade, mounted on its opalescent glazing. What are we meant to see in this quotation of a masterpiece of the Dutch Golden Age, famous to the point of being a stereotype? A fond or ironic/sarcastic cultural reminiscence? A melancholy evocation of quiet domesticity, set apart from the world, untouched by the anxieties of modernity? A nod to the voyeurism inherent in Vermeer's pictorial approach, and its *mise-en-abyme* with the fantastical intrusion

Lower-level room and rear garden

Lower-level curtains

into the intimacy of the villa that Koolhaas conjures up for us in *S,M,L,XL*? Or does the painting represent a kind of entry, via the Delft blue that is so strategically applied by the painter, into the innumerable resonances of this colour in the history of art? There is of course the blue of David Hockney, portraitist of Californian swimming pools and the bodies that animate them, and an artist whose universe is certainly not absent from *S,M,L,XL*'s pictorial tour. Then there are the blues of the avant-garde, the blue of Georges Bataille's sky, *Le Bleu du ciel*, the blue of Yves Klein, whose work

Koolhaas – breaking with habit – cites as having had an impact on his own.[15] Or why not, quite simply, the blue ink of the letter sent to the architect by the client for the villa, an apparently superfluous detail mentioned a few pages earlier?[16] From one strange thing to the next, this virtual promenade triggers speculations, each one as far-fetched and as plausible as the next, deployed in unstable, endlessly branching constructions, in sets of nesting conjectures. The villa is a *machine à imaginer*.

Both the angles of the images and their ambience reinforce the allusions to modernism that are threaded through the design of the villa. We recognise the suspended prisms pierced by the long ribbon bays of purist-era Le Corbusier, followed in turn by the glass boxes of Mies and Philip Johnson – Charles Jencks speaks of a *'cadavre exquis'*[17] – all patent references to which Koolhaas himself has drawn attention, as if to silence others.[18] The shifted volumes of the street facade and strange pivoted side wall might bring to mind the House of Dr Curutchet in La Plata,[19] or at least the model of it Le Corbusier presented in a well-known photograph. The gliding fabric of the drapes in the living space recalls the sumptuous hangings designed by Lilly Reich for the Villa Tugendhat ('All of Mies's later work used silk, velvet and leather as supple counter-architectures', Koolhaas writes just a few pages before this in *S,M,L,XL*).[20] The atmosphere also recalls some of the more marginal or deviant modernism of the interwar period. The fluted bamboo behind the perfectly smooth glass, the folded plastic wall of the kitchen set above the delicately speckled floor, the silk of the curtains against the grain of the concrete – these

View from elevated front bedroom towards the rear garden

piquant juxtapositions of sensuality and coldness, dandyism and asceticism, evoke the sophisticated associations and lascivious, decadent pile-ups that permeate the universe of Carlo Mollino. The Turin architect also used theatrical devices in photographing his interiors: this 'creative documentation' of his artificial worlds would eventually be published, but it was in the first instance directed towards self-exploration.[21]

If the images of the villa in *S,M,L,XL* look like stills from a movie set, it's because they are all effectively from a one-week shoot that took place in 1991, just before the owners moved in. Out of the shoot, photographed by Hans Werlemann and the videomaker Chiel van der Stelt, came a 12-minute film, titled *2042: The Villa dall'Ava by OMA* (1992), directed and edited by Claudi Cornaz, who was also an active member of Rotterdam's artistic avant-garde and a preferred collaborator of OMA at the time.[22] Its *mise-en-scène* was guided by little scenarios: 'the idea was to test the perennial qualities of the villa by imagining it in 20 situations 50 years from now', Werlemann explained.[23] 'The basic idea is that the villa offers its inhabitants

---

Hendrick Goltzius, Farnese Hercules, 1592

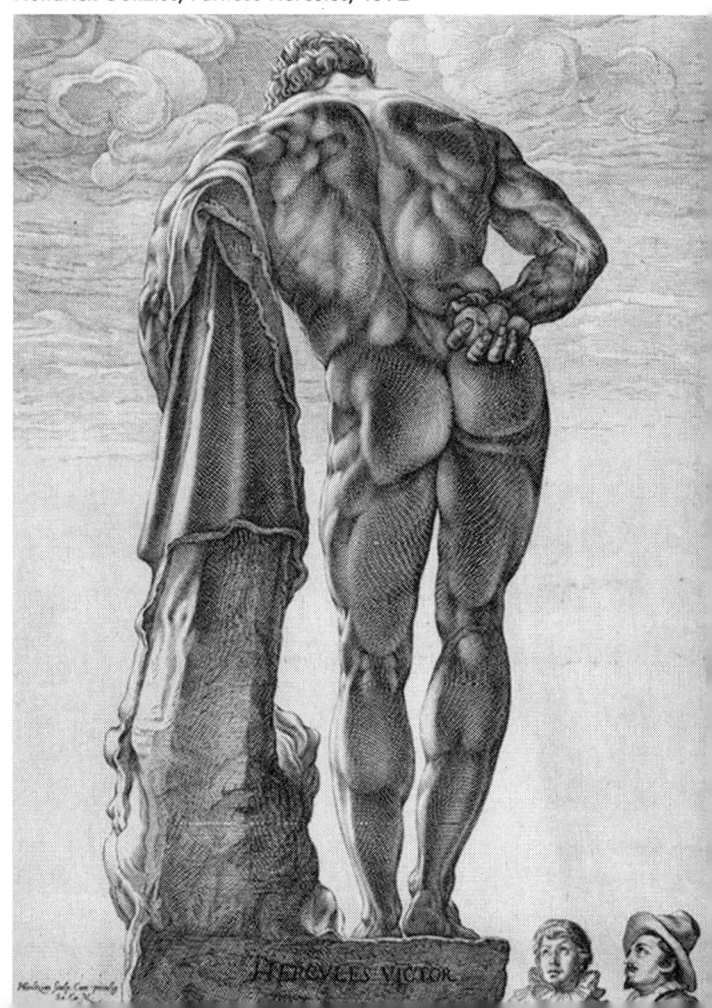

Hendrick Goltzius, The Fall of Phaeton, 1588

Showering Villa dall'Ava bathers, 1991

Bruce Bellas, physique model posing as a cowboy, 1959

Upper-level bathroom

'Bigness', with a Bruce Bellas photograph, S,M,L,XL, 1995

Michelangelo Antonioni, L'Eclisse, 1962

protection from the overwhelming influences and events on the outside, which only penetrate in through the media.'[24] Conceived as an antidote to the clichés of architectural photography, the images appeared first in published reviews of the building and were then reused in *S,M,L,XL*. Though the film itself was somehow forgotten – it would not be screened for almost 30 years – the ambience of the photographs made an immediate and lasting impression when they appeared in publications, influencing the way we have looked at the villa ever since.[25]

The images selected for the book are saturated with references to the history of cinema. A checklist might include the movies of Hitchcock's American period (the voyeurism of *Rear Window*, the phobias of *Vertigo*) and those films that capture the involuntary burlesque of modern environments (*Mon Oncle* by Jacques Tati) or their underlying pathologies. Koolhaas has also acknowledged the influence of the 'sceptical,

disillusioned modernity' of Italian cinema of the 1960s.[26] The skulking presence here is the trio of films Antonioni made with Monica Vitti, where the characters look for, brush up against and then lose each other in ordinary places that are transmuted by the director into surreal settings. Think, for example, of the opening of *L'Eclisse*, a film full of paradoxical symmetries. A woman breaks up with her lover within the confines of an apartment that becomes more and more suffocating as the night wears on. The scene ends at dawn, when she draws back the curtains to reveal the mute landscape of the EUR district of Rome. The film then takes Vitti into the frantic clamour of the stock exchange, where she meets the stockbroker played by Alain Delon. Antonioni's editing of the scene equates Italy's urban modernisation with the financial activity that produces landscapes which are just as disembodied as it is. Might the insertion of the shouting Parisian trader into the pages of *S,M,L,XL* hark back to this idea?[27]

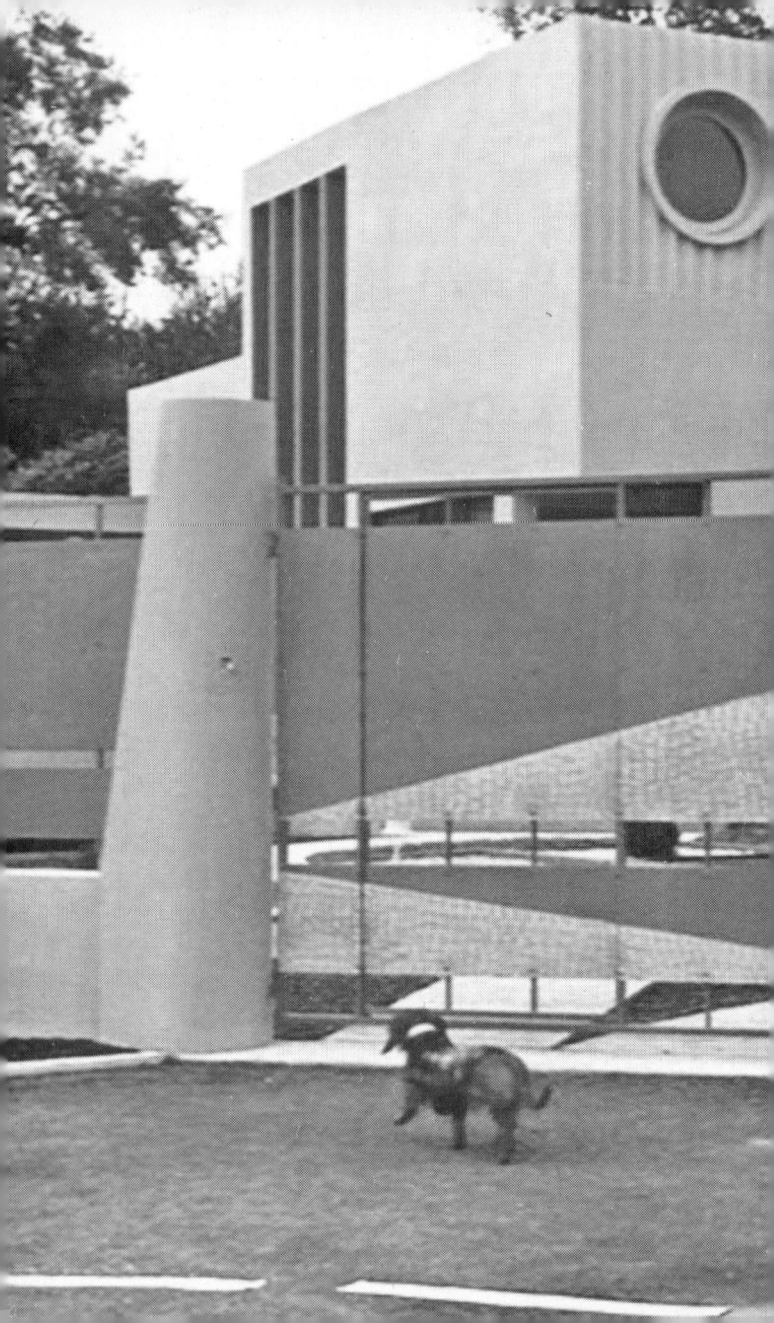

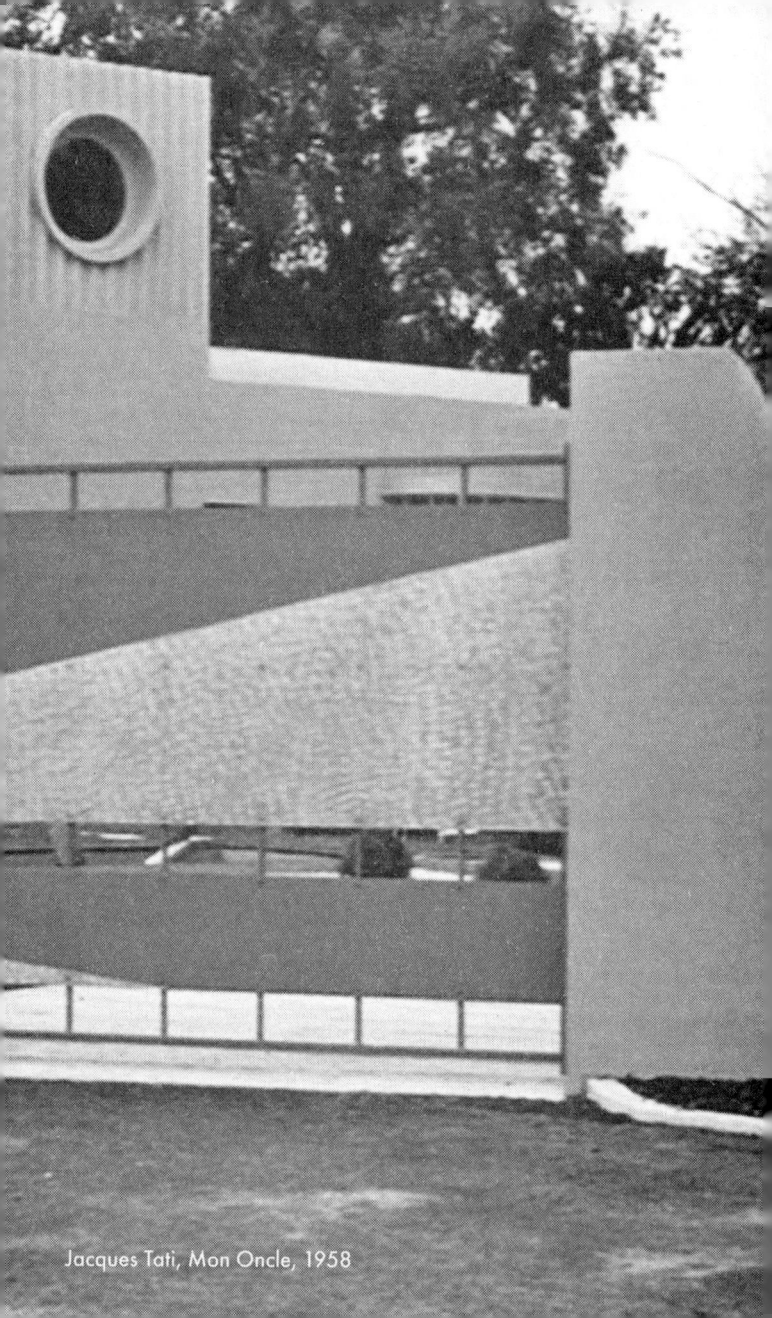

Jacques Tati, Mon Oncle, 1958

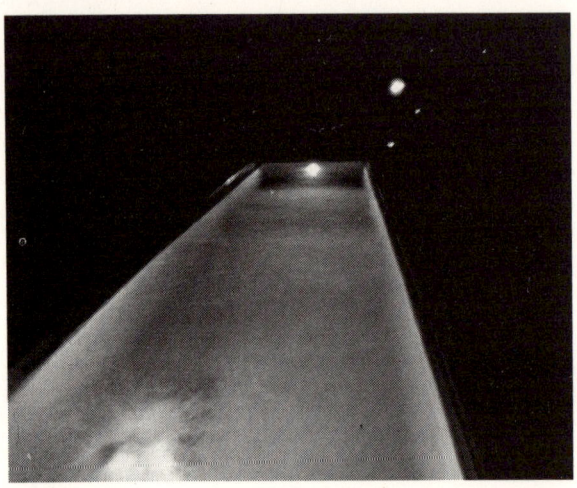
Rooftop pool

The climax of the book's promenade through the Villa dall'Ava – the rooftop pool where the daytime flurry of swimmers gives way, at dusk, to a woman immersed in the water, fully clothed, leaning pensively against the edge of the pool, before night falls and the strip of water, finally emptied of all human presence, lights up Paris like a cinema ramp – brings to mind a few other famous films featuring bathing places. Cinema has long turned this emblem of the pleasures of water and physical exercise into theatre: a setting for primal terror (*Cat People*, Jacques Tourneur), crimes of passion (*Sunset Boulevard*, Billy Wilder), cheerful despair (*La Notte*, Michelangelo Antonioni; *The Swimmer*, Frank Perry), dreamed eroticism (*Deep End*, Jerzy Skolimowski), troubled hedonism (*A Bigger Splash*, Jack Hazan), or unhealthy obsession (*Heat*,

Frank Perry, The Swimmer, 1968

Billy Wilder, Sunset Boulevard, 1950

Michelangelo Antonioni, La Notte, 1961

Jacques Tourneur, Cat People, 1942

Jerzy Skolimowski, Deep End, 1970

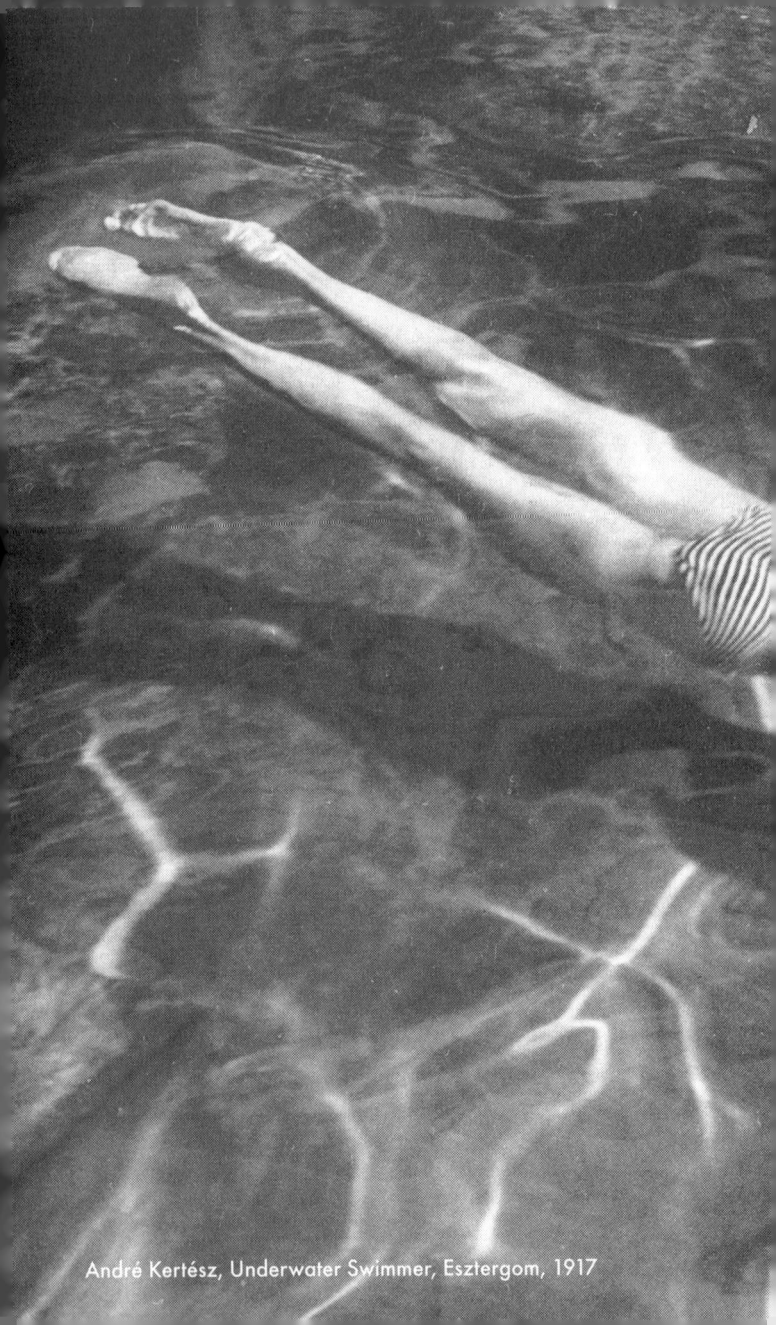
André Kertész, Underwater Swimmer, Esztergom, 1917

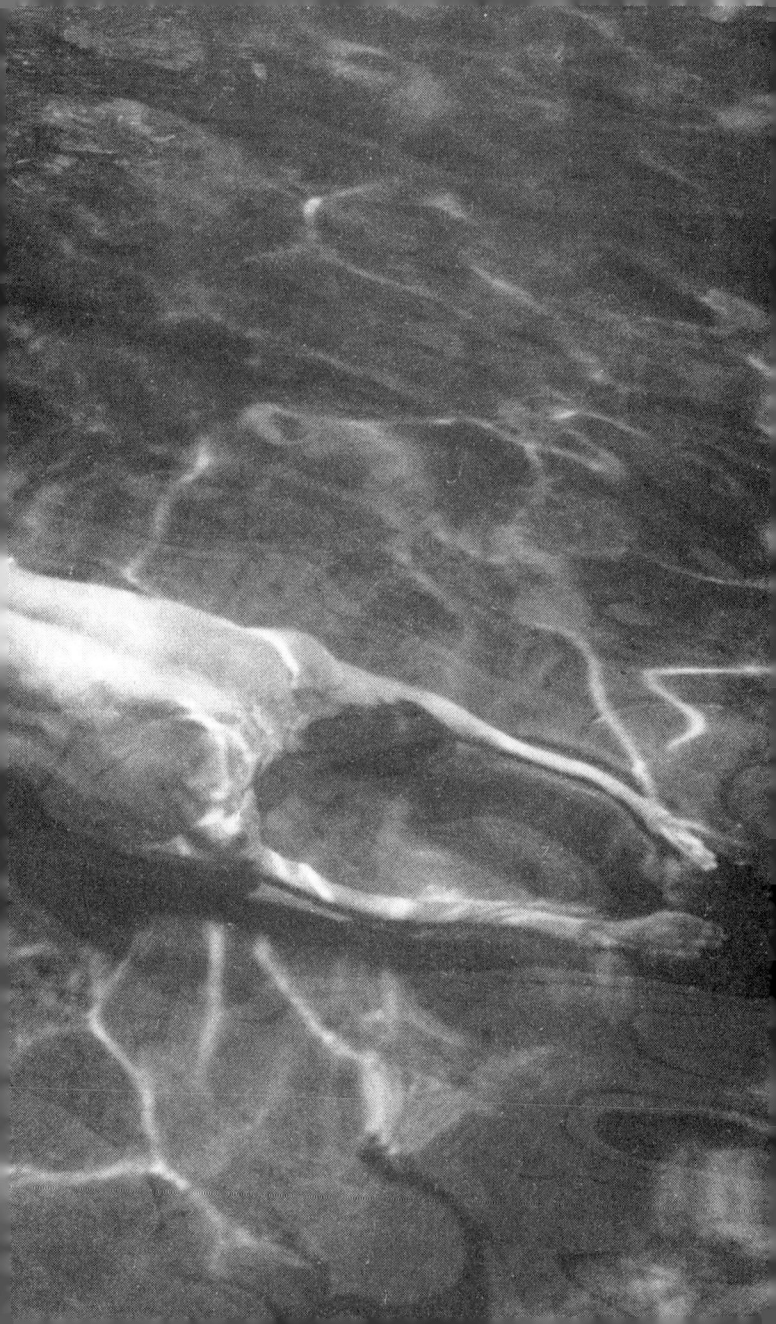

David Hockney, Portrait of an Artist (Pool with Two Figures), 1972

Paul Morrissey, with Joe Dalessandro – a belated parody of *Sunset Boulevard* enacted by sulphurous protagonists of the New York underground). From André Kertész's photograph of a swimmer whose contours are dissolved by the shimmering ripples he creates on the water (*Underwater Swimmer, Esztergom, Hungary*, 1917) to David Hockney's *Portrait of an Artist (Pool with Two Figures)*, (1972), from Max Ernst's metaphysical *Aquis submersus* (1919) to de Chirico's *Bain mystérieux* (1938) and the series of deserted pools in Ed Ruscha's *Nine Swimming Pools* (1968), the theme of the pool and its magnetic blue runs through the entire history of modern art, from the avant-gardes to pop art.

As for the wholesale mobilising of a house to turn it into the protagonist of a fiction, this inevitably evokes the part played by the Casa Malaparte in Jean-Luc

Max Ernst, Aquis submersus, 1919

Ed Ruscha, Nine Swimming Pools, 1968

Godard's *Le Mépris*.[28] The (mis)quotation with which the director opens the film – 'Cinema, said André Bazin, substitutes for the real world one that accords more closely with our desires' – could even serve as an epigraph for Werlemann's oneiric transmutation of the Villa dall'Ava. The *Monditalia* exhibition at the 2014 Venice Architecture Biennale featured excerpts from *Le Mépris*, as well as an installation dedicated to the Italian writer's villa.[29] The island of Capri – since ancient times a place where a privileged few have come to enjoy the pleasures of vacation, freed for a while from the obligations of city life – was portrayed as a 'symbol of exuberance and unfulfilled desires', a thwarted utopia.[30] Like that villa and so many other modern houses before it, might the Villa dall'Ava be re-enacting in its own way this push and pull between the intimate refuge and the metropolis?

Finally, in a deliberate anticlimax (or seeming attempt to dispel) the disquieting sorcery of the images, the last pages of the chapter in *S,M,L,XL* present the plans, sections and elevations of the villa. Here again, the format is disconcerting: black-and-white working drawings annotated by architect in red ballpoint pen.

Jean-Luc Godard, Le Mépris, 1963

Section and elevation, Villa dall'Ava, S,M,L,XL, 1995
(above and overleaf)

ngs on
ching the
rain,
with
idual

```
          6400
  tôle ondulée finition cuivre
  isolant 80 mm.
  béton armé 200 mm.
  peinture
          5320*

  parquet chêne
  béton armé 200 mm.
  plafonds de plaques de plâtre
          4420*
          3080*
          2900*

          2100*

  chape epoxy
  chauffage par le sol 40 mm.
  isolant 40 mm.
  béton armé 200 mm.
          +000

  béton armé étanche
  isolant 80 mm.
  stub 20 mm.

  chape béton de finition
  béton armé 200 mm.
          -1520*
```

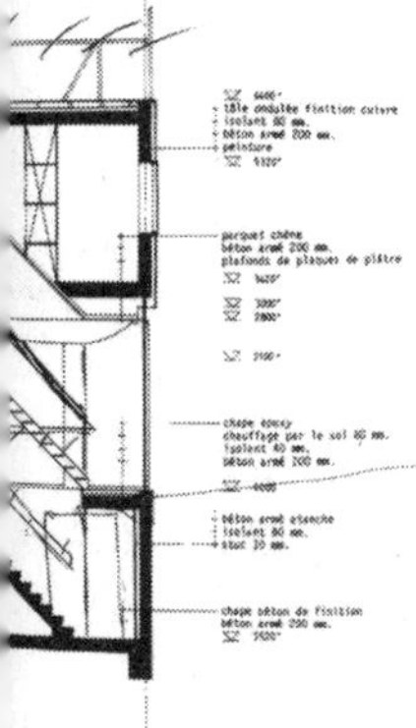

rizontal lines
l horrible in
ring room
one 'stick' left

The house is actually positioned in an incredibly complex, dense situation. It is about its relationship with its neighbours, its context. The best way to represent it would be to take the house as a frame to describe its environment. <u>It is not an object!</u>

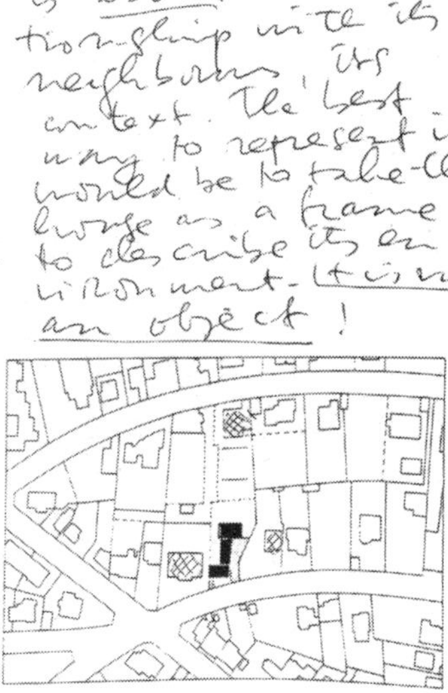

The collision between the disciplinary dryness of these architectural representations and the volubility of the handwritten commentary, which is by turns explanatory, assertive and prescriptive, turns the spotlight on the creative process, on the means that are used to shape a future reality on paper. This graphic approach sets up a tension between the objective distance established by the orthographic projection drawings and the tactile quality and feigned immediacy of the handwriting, which is immaculately reproduced on the surface of the printed page.[31] The notes appear to have been written after the event on an intermediate version of the plans, so as to make it easier to retrospectively trace the impact of these remarks and instructions on the work one has just seen. The railings, for example, have been vigorously crossed out in red hatching ('I hate the ship metaphor. Railings are very hard to do without resurrecting the liners from the 20s') as a way of explaining their absence, and the vertigo of a visit to the rooftop.[32] These handwritten notes offer a strategic distillation of information on architectural intentions, something the opening text, 'Obstacles', pointedly avoids. Koolhaas delivers pithy insights into the genesis of his project, after showing its built form through screen grabs of a film that imagines its future state.

The whole *S,M,L,XL* presentation thus rearranges the chronology of the project in a way that blurs registers: first, we have the scenario – but it's for a retrospective fable; then comes the storyboard – for a prospective film; and finally the drawings – of what has just been shown as a completed building. Writing, film, architecture: how could one fail to notice that the sequence

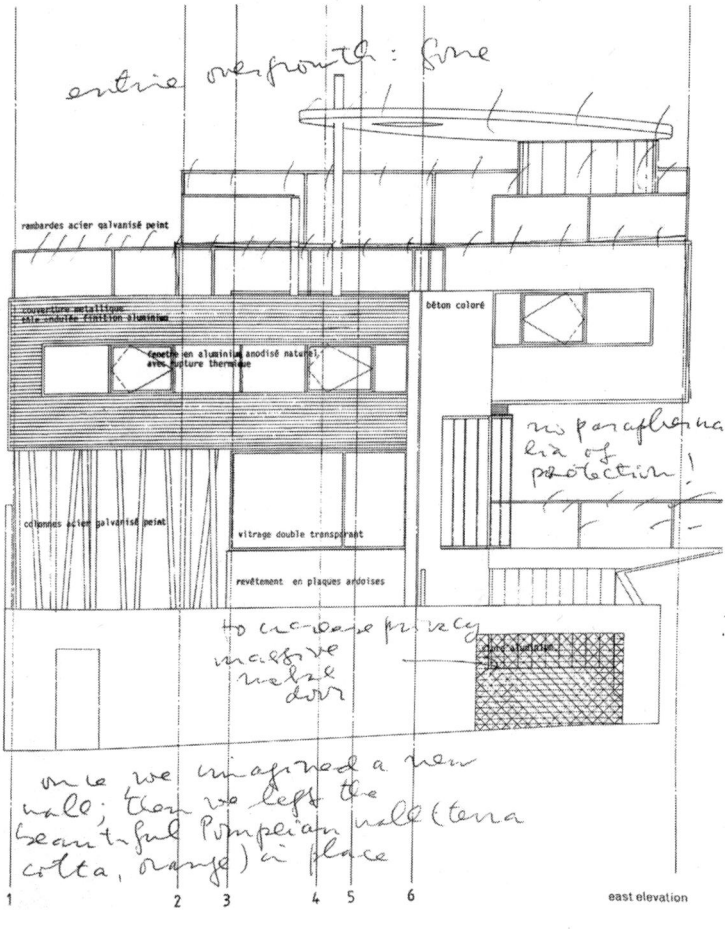

in which the villa is presented mirrors the stages of its designer's career? As everyone knows, Koolhaas was, at 19, a journalist for the cultural pages of a general-interest weekly, and then a screenwriter, before he embarked on his studies at the Architectural Association in London, cofounding OMA five years later.[33] Going back to his family tree, these professions correspond to those of his father, Anton Koolhaas, a journalist, writer, critic, producer and director of the Dutch Film Academy, and his grandfather, Dirk Roosenburg, an architect. The *casa come me* is how Malaparte described his villa on Capri, a house that resembled him so much that he titled the text he wrote about it 'Ritratto di pietra' (Portrait in Stone). A study that appeared to take this premise literally, questioning the usual attribution of the design to Adalberto Libera, caused quite a stir in architectural circles in the 1990s. Upturning the official account, historian Marida Talamona used documentary evidence to establish that the architecture of the villa owed a great deal to Malaparte himself, in the process resolving questions about certain elements that had been difficult to associate with the architect credited with their design. Born, like its predecessor, from the imagination of a writer-screenwriter-architect, woven out of personal references drawn from the entire history of modern art, could the Villa dall'Ava also be a reflection, a mirror, a self-portrait of its designer? A *casa come lui*?[34]

WAYWARD SAVOYE

Let's keep this hypothesis at the back of our minds while we take a look at the last spread in the series. Curiously, this is a black-and-white shot of the garden facade taken when the building was only a raw concrete carcass. Often in architectural monographs, an image of the construction site is inserted into the presentation of the successive phases of a project as a way of testifying to its *progress* towards its final form. Here it appears as a last flashback, a Parthian shot, a final *coup de théâtre* before the curtain falls. And since the same facade was shown a few pages earlier from an identical angle, all decked out in its extravagant finery – the raspberry-coloured corrugated siding, the large planes of glass, the bamboo – this final reformulation of the chronology of the building gives the impression that its splendid outer layer has simply *disappeared*. Stripped of its cladding, the concrete prism of the garden floor extends in all its lumpy minerality across the width of the double page, its symmetry restored by the central line of supports exposed by the omission of the building envelope.

Why does Koolhaas show us the building stripped bare in this way? Is it to give us a glimpse behind the scenes of the project? Or to emphasise the crudeness of the activity of construction, to recall the base material to make clear everything the architect has to do before he can work his magic? Or is this final, rather cruel manipulation an attempt to dissolve the charm and open our eyes to the reality? That possibility recalls

Villa dall'Ava, S,M,L,XL, 1995

the opening scenario in *S,M,L,XL*: to be an architect, Koolhaas insists, is ultimately to be a kind of hero – and I'm proving it. Could it be that he is whispering, not without a hint of malice, a clue about the lineage of the building and therefore about the intention behind it? For the *undressed* villa reveals the raw truth that had been concealed by its cladding and make-up. With the lights doused, the spell broken, the flamboyant actress lets slip her mask and reveals the old lady behind it. Poking out from behind, or rather beneath, the Villa dall'Ava is the subliminal image of one of the 'intimidations' that is acknowledged in the opening scenario but – it suddenly seems very clear – in fact haunts all the images: the Villa Savoye.

Parallels have often been drawn between the two houses. Writing in *L'Architecture d'Aujourd'hui* soon after the villa's completion, the critic Jean-Paul Robert was probably the first to evoke its silhouette 'reminiscent of an aggressive and run-down Villa Savoye', its 'floor torn by a long window, set on a floating ground level that stands on piles'. For his part, Richard Ingersoll saw in these 'drunken piloti ... an amusing provocation, whether one is familiar with Le Corbusier's problems of placing his columns in Villa Savoye or not'.[35] Since then, there has not been a single essay or graphic reconstruction of the villa posted on the internet by a student of architecture anywhere on the planet that does not refer to these similarities in one way or another. However, looking more closely, beyond these stylistic borrowings or circumstantial analogies, there are much more profound connections between the villas of Koolhaas and Le Corbusier. The five points of a new architecture are all present in the Villa dall'Ava, albeit in a distorted form, twisted to the point of irrationality – and it is this spectacle of their systematic misuse that Koolhaas is inviting us to witness. Independent frame? Rather than being a stable prism lifted from the ground by a legible regular structure, the raised volume is cut in two halves, which are then arranged in the shape of a hand-crank and maintained in a shaky equilibrium by a central structure that is encased in an interior facade – deliberately made illegible. Pilotis? Too many on one side, not enough on the other. On the side facing the street, a forest of poles supports the upper floor, or ties it to the ground – who knows which – while the only thing that seems to prevent the lopsided garden apartment from toppling over is the meagre post that props it up at the far end. Freely designed facade? Horizontal window? With Le Corbusier, the framework of the

Pilotis, Villa Savoye, 1931

Pilotis, Villa dall'Ava, 1991

Living room, Villa Savoye, 1931

Ramp, Villa Savoye, 1931

Living room, Villa dall'Ava, 1991

Ramp, Villa dall'Ava, 1991

Roof terrace, Villa Savoye, 1931

Kitchen, Villa Savoye, 1931

Roof terrace, Villa dall'Ava, 1990

Kitchen, Villa dall'Ava, 1990

glazing is continuous and symmetrical; with Koolhaas, a concrete shear wall brutally truncates the street facade and horizontal window, delivering a body blow to the alignment. Free plan? Le Corbusier explored the effects of uncoupling the internal organisation from the loadbearing constraints; in the Villa dall'Ava Koolhaas pushes this uncoupling to the point of making the domestic uses practically nomadic. Released from its utilitarian chores, the plan promotes a generalised *dérive* in which function is accommodated only reluctantly. There are three armchairs indicating the presence of a living room, but nothing to suggest that people can gather here. The kitchen seems to be hanging around in a hallway. The study has taken refuge in the basement, where the single light socket punctures the ceiling like a hole in a trepanned skull. Roof terrace? In the place of the 'dry, salubrious' cloister prescribed by Le Corbusier,[36] what we find up there is the swimming pool, a water-filled hollow beam that holds the structure together, extended by a lichen-covered platform and an orange plastic mesh fence impersonating railings. 'Sun bathing', announced Le Corbusier in the *Oeuvre complète*;[37] 'midnight dip', replies Koolhaas in *S,M,L,XL*, with his picture of a pensive woman immersed fully clothed in the pool, enveloped in the artificial half-light of a cinematic day-for-night.

As a consequence, the architectural promenade, which in Le Corbusier describes a spatial composition experienced in a continuous tracking shot, becomes, when revised by Koolhaas, an agglomeration of singular spaces skewered by paths of circulation. Repatriated inside the envelope, the Corbusian ramp contracts into

Ramp under construction, 1990

an inclined plane, or rather a steeply sloping strip that extends from the lower entrance to the living room, from where it hands over to metal flights of stairs that trace a looping route up to the two apartments and the pool. The exquisite corpse is also a palindrome, or a Moebius strip, perhaps.[38] The key invention of cinema – montage – makes it possible to fabricate a continuous narrative out of autonomous 'takes' in time and space. In the same way, Koolhaas sets out to assemble a coherent spatial narrative from discontinuous spatial fragments – both in reality, in the house, as well as in the 'visual tour' offered in the book. Even his frontal views reverse the logic behind Le Corbusier's choice of photographs to represent the villa in the *Oeuvre complète*. With Le Corbusier, there is a perspectival mode of composition that Thomas Schumacher has suggested corresponds to that of Piero della Francesca's *The Flagellation*;[39] the mostly asymmetrical framing of the views aims at visually fixing the dynamics of the fluid, harmonious spatial relations set up by the plan. With Koolhaas, the symmetrical views enhance by contrast collisions, angular shapes and the precarious relation to gravity of the volumes they depict.

Variations on Le Corbusier as both a source and a target continue in the drawings. The longitudinal section of the Villa dall'Ava, extending over a full double-page spread of *S,M,L,XL*, appears to be modelled on that of the Villa Savoye, except that the *poché* of the upper sloping plane indicates the bottom of the pool rather than the penultimate flight of the ramp. The commentary on the site plan, which appears as a vignette in the corner of another page, insists heavily on the contextual nature of the intervention: 'The house is actually positioned in an incredibly complex, dense situation. It is *about* its relationship with its neighbours... *It is not* an object!',[40] Koolhaas exclaims, in a term-for-term reversal of the caption to the distant view of the Villa Savoye in the *Oeuvre complète*: 'The house is an object placed above the ground, in the middle of the landscape.'[41]

Might that dense but ordinary suburban setting be the way to reconnect early modernism with reality, to free it from its indifference to anything other than theoretical constraints and thus give it a new lease of life?

Furthermore, it's not just the photographs, drawings and words, but the whole model of *S,M,L,XL*, with its iconographic choices, that seems designed to outdo Le Corbusier's efforts to break away from the traditional format of the book, with his use of visual montages inspired by 'vernacular' publications such as commercial catalogues or advertisements. Le Corbusier also saw his books 'as intellectual as well as material projects'; he, too, liked to 'control every aspect of their production from A to Z'.[42] Already in 1924, in an ad for *Vers une architecture*, he declared: 'This book draws its eloquence from new means, with its superb illustrations unfolding a powerful discourse in parallel with the text. This new conception of the book, where the illustrations play an explicitly instructive and expository role, enables the author to avoid meaningless descriptions.'[43] With his project for *S,M,L,XL*, Koolhaas seems to be picking up where Le Corbusier left off, summoning from his own time the means to deftly sidestep the paralysis of commentary. 'Exploiting technological advances in printing, *S,M,L,XL* ... creates an artificial and fantastic space out of nearly every spread of the book.'[44] Just as advances in technology, and in particular the introduction of the elevator, allowed for the emergence in Manhattan of a new type of metropolitan object, the skyscraper – as Koolhaas recalls a few pages further on, in his essay on 'Bigness' – so the application of digital technology to publishing has made it possible to create a visual space where the reader can move at will from one spread to another, as if they were navigating the different levels of one of those 'cities within the city'.

Thus, in reality as well as in his representation, Koolhaas methodically tortures each of the ideas tested by Le Corbusier in the 1920s, stretching them to breaking point in order to extract their untapped potential. A form of crash test, in sum, but also of appropriation, a homage and at the same time a challenge to an oedipal duel, an eye for an eye (and a point for a point). The Villa dall'Ava has all the traits of a Villa Savoye that has been cannibalised, perverted by this Sadean/sadistic conversion of an emblem of purism into an obscure object of desire. Rather than invoking concepts or dogmas, Koolhaas justifies his strategy in terms of logistical constraints (programme, budget, regulations, context), which only serves to confuse our gauge of reason still further. Another layer can be added, then, to the interpretation of the framing of Paris in the *S,M,L,XL* site photo. What lies midway between the Villa dall'Ava and the Eiffel Tower, at the centre of the spread, in the crease of the binding, is of course Le Corbusier's first villa in Paris, Maison La Roche – in other words, the guardian of the temple, the Fondation Le Corbusier on square du Dr Blanche.[45]

How to understand this covert – but also voluntarist, as well as ambivalent – reinterpretation of the principles of modern architecture based on Le Corbusier's most famous, most expository villa? In line with the adage that 'bad architects borrow, good architects steal', we could perhaps see this as Koolhaas praising cannibalism as the right way to appropriate the master's works, while taunting contemporary attempts which merely paraphrase them. This would hark back to one of the hottest debates of the late 1960s, when the New York Five attempted to reclaim, and in the process re-legitimise, the basic elements of the vocabulary of early modern architecture. The book that first presented them as a group, brought together by Arthur Drexler, was published in 1972, the year Koolhaas arrived in New York after graduating from the Architectural Association (AA) in London. At the Institute for Architectural and Urban Studies (IAUS) – his base when he was writing *Delirious New York* – these 'ruminations on Le Corbusier were absorbed in a cyclical logic of "autonomous" reflection, bordering on idolatry'.[46] Could Koolhaas's sarcastic reinvention of Corbusian principles also be a strategy to bypass the deference shown by the powerful neo-purist tendency, a dominant force in French architecture in the years the villa was being designed? Led by Henri Ciriani and his UNO group at the Paris-Belleville school of architecture, battalions of young designers were trained in the mechanics of 'modern space', inculcated with a fastidious, even dogmatic fidelity to the precepts of the modern movement, which was understood as a 'new tradition', in the sense defined by Sigfried Giedion.

Rather than deification or reverence, Koolhaas has always inclined towards iconoclastic love – for example, by the installation OMA created for the 17th Milan Triennale, just before the project for the villa, which broached Mies's 1929 Barcelona Pavilion and the problem of its contemporary relevance. At the time (1986), 'a clone of the Mies pavilion was being built in Barcelona', writes Koolhaas in *S,M,L,XL*. 'How fundamentally', he asks, 'did it differ from Disney? In the name of a higher authenticity, we researched the true history of the pavilion after the closing of the 1929 World's Fair and collected whatever archaeological remnants it has left across Europe on its return journey. Like a Pompeian villa, these fragments were reassembled as far as possible to suggest the former whole, but with one inevitable inaccuracy: since our "site" was curved, the pavilion had to be "bent".'[47] Bent, that is, twisted in plan to fit the exhibition space that OMA had been assigned in the apse of the Palazzo della Triennale, but also bent (perverted) by a radical reversal of its original emptiness. Overprogrammed with sports activities, OMA's reinterpretation was transformed into a 'Bodybuilding House' or 'Casa Palestra', referring to an omnipresent theme in avant-garde architecture, physical culture.[48] 'It has always been our conviction that modern architecture is a hedonistic movement', Koolhaas writes on this subject, 'that its abstraction, rigor and severity are in fact plots to create the most provocative settings for the experiment that is modern life'.[49] How, then, should one understand the symbolic twist on Le Corbusier supplied by the parodic architecture of the villa?

Is Koolhaas revisiting the basic elements of the language of modern architecture in his own way, rearranging them so as to destabilise their established equilibrium, to subvert their hierarchies? This was an agenda shared by the 'deconstructivism' he would be associated with in the wake of the 1988 MoMA exhibition.[50] But the Villa dall'Ava was not among the works that represented OMA at the show, even though the project was wrapped up by then. Or is the intention, as Emmanuel Petit has suggested, to demonstrate, 'in a quite didactic way, his rhetorical play with modern architecture, now fathomed as a "language" readily available for reformulations and elaboration'?[51] Alternatively, could this be an attempt to re-enact, with the canons of modernism, the deliberately licentious subversion of the vocabulary of the classical orders effected by mannerism in its own time?[52] Nikolaus Pevsner saw in that wilful assault on Renaissance aesthetic values the desire to create a critical architecture, one that echoed the turmoil experienced by artists living in a violent age. And the way mannerist architects sought to achieve this, according to Pevsner, was to literally dissolve the ideals of formal balance and harmony of proportions, the touchstones of Renaissance art. Bruno Zevi, and then Manfredo Tafuri, were able to draw parallels between that expression of a period of crisis and the architecture of their own time.[53] Is Koolhaas likewise – as a keen observer and insatiable commentator of the contemporary cultural condition – seeking to express in architecture the disorder of the century, its 'terrifying beauty', to use his phrase, and so create his own 'construction of *merveilles*', to borrow the fine subtitle given by Roberto Gargiani to his monograph on OMA?

This hypothesis is (retroactively) lent some credence by one of the few personally signed interventions in 'Koolhaas's' Venice Biennale in 2014, where he returned to a 2006 visit to Michelangelo's Laurentian Library in Florence, in a short text accompanied by a mosaic of photographs of the vestibule taken by his daughter Charlie.[54] Evoking the experience of this space, which was 'terrifying, almost like a nightmare', where 'nothing worked' but 'the sum of all its dysfunctionalities was gripping', Koolhaas seems to be retrospectively describing what he himself did to the canons of purism with his villa: 'Michelangelo takes each architectural element and forces it into new shapes and new relationships – he respects no rules and ridicules the "lessons" architects have applied to their own profession. He breaks down and reimagines the wall, the window and the door in an area no bigger than a living room, dominated by a huge sculpture that pretends to be a staircase.'[55] Would Koolhaas do the same to the modernist 'orders' with the Villa dall'Ava, a building no bigger than a house? As a mannerist object, the villa would anchor OMA in the lineage of a critical modernity that was born with modernity itself, via a long-unloved period in history and an often-disparaged style that was set on the road to a controversial rehabilitation by Robert Venturi and Denise Scott Brown's rereading from the late 1960s.[56] Beyond the famous argument of *Complexity and Contradiction in Architecture*, and before Venturi and Scott Brown's claims for a new mannerism, there was the Vanna Venturi House (1959–64), where a pediment morphs into a gabled facade, an uncanny fusion of a classical and a vernacular reference into a new, ambiguous element.[57] 'I think it's a harvesting of some of the remnants [of modernism] that are left in a kind of collective consciousness. For me it's an interesting point where modernity maybe is almost a vernacular', Koolhaas said after a presentation of the Villa dall'Ava in the US in 1986.[58] Does this make the little house in Saint-Cloud a device that would help to

Charlie Koolhaas, Biblioteca Laurenziana, Venice Biennale, 2014

rebuild modernism by accelerating its absorption into mainstream culture, in line with Koolhaas's reading of the history of Manhattan, his previous contribution to the contemporary debate? It was there, he argued, that a form of architecture had developed that was 'at once ambitious *and* popular', and whose *a posteriori* theorisation should 'deliver the formula': that unconscious ideology he brought to light and dubbed 'Manhattanism'.[59] Or, responding more directly to current debates in architecture, might the villa also be read as an attack on Colin Rowe's famous comparison of Le Corbusier's villa at Garches and Palladio's 'La Malcontenta', based on similarities in the composition of their plans?[60] Koolhaas's distrust of Rowe's historicist formalism is well known.[61] Is his intention to bring to life in this small house the *folie* of purism that remained latent in Le Corbusier's villa – to reveal its *potential* mannerism, as opposed to its actual reduction to a form of classicism? If so, the Villa dall'Ava project would have a dual aim: to counter postmodernism, which sought to revive reassuring ties with the past at the risk of getting mired in historicism; and to draw a line under the failings of modernism, looking instead to resurrect modernity by unleashing its fertile ambiguities.

FLAGRANT DALÍ

With these questions in mind, let's go back to the images of the villa published by OMA. The office website highlights a photograph that does not feature in the pages of *S,M,L,XL*. So often reproduced that it has become an icon, it shows the terrace and its swimming pool at dusk, on axis with the Eiffel Tower, which is lit up in the distance. In the foreground of the picture stands a statuesque swimmer in black swimsuit and cap, bending forward with her arms outstretched and preparing to dive – though it's not clear quite how she'll manage this without hurting herself as she's facing the long side of the pool. This absurd, beguiling vision, credited to the photographer Peter Aaron, echoes another series of images taken by Hans Werlemann during the one-week shoot at the villa, showing simulated aquatic romps alongside a nocturnal scene on the terrace, with characters in costume. Dressed in one-piece swimsuits reminiscent of 1920s beachwear, the OMA staff requisitioned for the occasion stand in a row on the edge of the pool, arms extended, in a demonstration of coordinated gymnastics.

The explicit reference for both Werlemann and Aaron here is of course 'The Story of the Pool', written by Koolhaas and illustrated by Madelon Vriesendorp.[62] Everyone remembers this tale of mythical constructivist architects/lifeguards who propel their floating swimming pool towards an idealised Manhattan, only to turn around in shock on reaching their destination – a parable of the disillusionment of utopia that served

Peter Aaron, Swimmer, 1991

'Curiosités parisiennes', 1910, postcard from the Dalí collection

Pierre Chenal, Architecture d'Aujourdhui, 1930

as a kind of coda to *Delirious New York*. The association of the villa with the image of that swimming pool focused on what was the emblem of Manhattan at the time – the twin towers of the World Trade Center – has also often been noted.[63] But then, the simulacrum of sporting choreography by the side of the Villa dall'Ava swimming pool could be seen as a further ironic allusion to Le Corbusier – and specifically a response to the early morning exercises on the roof terrace of the villa at Garches filmed by Pierre Chenal in his short, *Architecture d'Aujourd'hui*.[64] We have Corb's edifying scene: an exposition of the simple pleasures of suburban life (a little exercise before setting off for work in town), with its rosy-cheeked hygienism (the whole family taking the fresh air on the rooftop garden) and instructive character (slightly undermined by the fact that Madame is wearing elegant high-heeled shoes to do her gymnastics). And OMA's retaliation: a ludic ballet of bachelors performing under the gaze of the metropolis at nightfall. The image also echoes Malaparte exercising on the flat roof terrace of his villa facing the sea: 'Here, every morning [he] would perform a ritual of

Villa dall'Ava bathers, 1991

The Aqua-Zanies performing at the Astoria Pool, New York, 1940

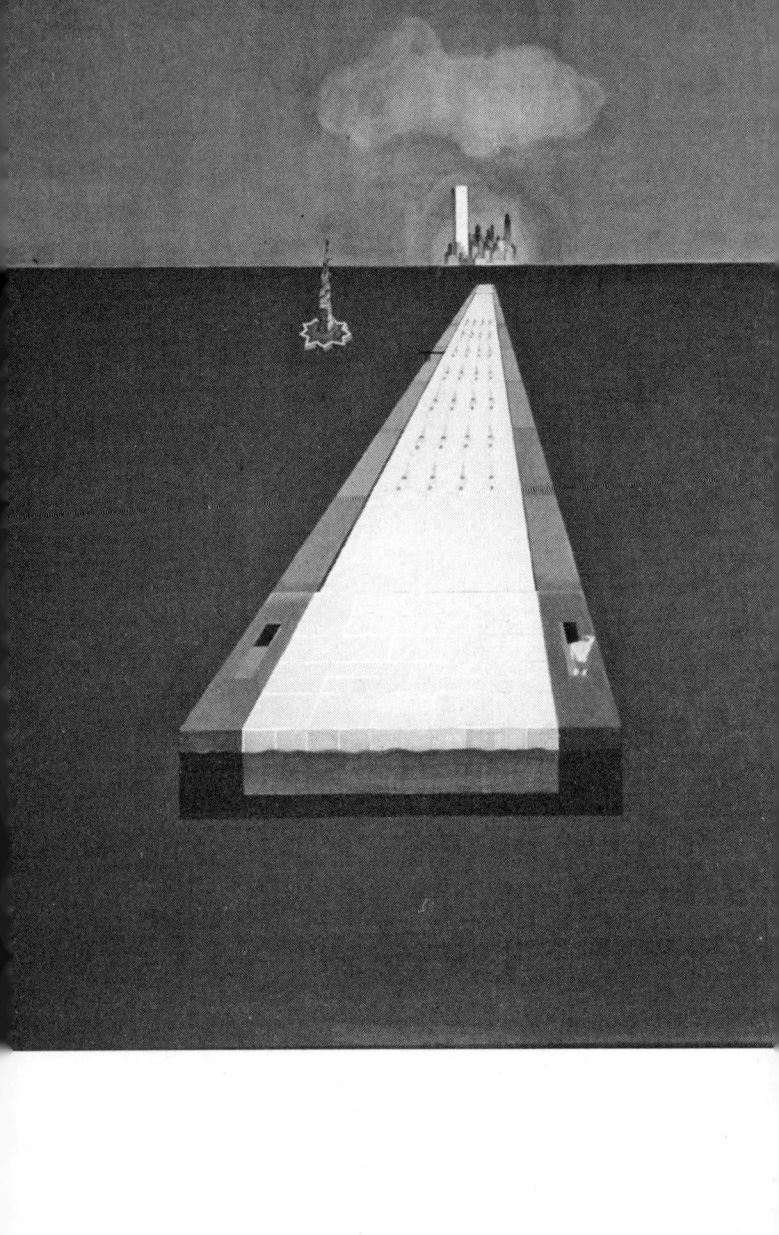

gymnastics, alone, while the women who were in love with him would watch from the cliffs above.'[65]

But more than anything else, Werlemann's poolside fiction, with its improvised cast in their retro costumes, brings to mind another cinematic short which slightly predates Chenal's: *Les Mystères du château de Dé*, filmed by Man Ray at the Villa Noailles at Hyères – another domestic masterpiece of the 1920s designed by another Parisian star of the modern movement, Robert Mallet-Stevens. The Noailles, noted protectors and patrons of the avant-garde and ardent promoters of surrealism, gave Man Ray carte blanche to make a film on their 'château' and their art collections, garnished with some shots of their 'guests disporting themselves in the swimming pool'.[66] Man Ray goes out of his way to make the house's geometric architecture look bizarre, framing its assemblies of cubes, the windows punched in the garden wall and the empty interiors in such a way that they smoulder with a feeling of strangeness. ('Where are we?' wonders one of the title cards.) In its winter garb, standing in isolation on a hill overlooking the sea, the Villa Noailles appears at once as a refuge and a threat – a sort of modernist pendant to the Château de Silling.[67]

The swimming scene comes as a playful interlude after this disturbing sequence. Lingering on the reflections produced by the water lapping against the walls, the camera captures the Noailles and their friends from every angle as they frolic in the water, dressed in striped bathing costumes, with black shorts and matching swimming caps, until they exit single file along the

Madelon Vriesendorp, The Arrival of the Floating Pool, 1975

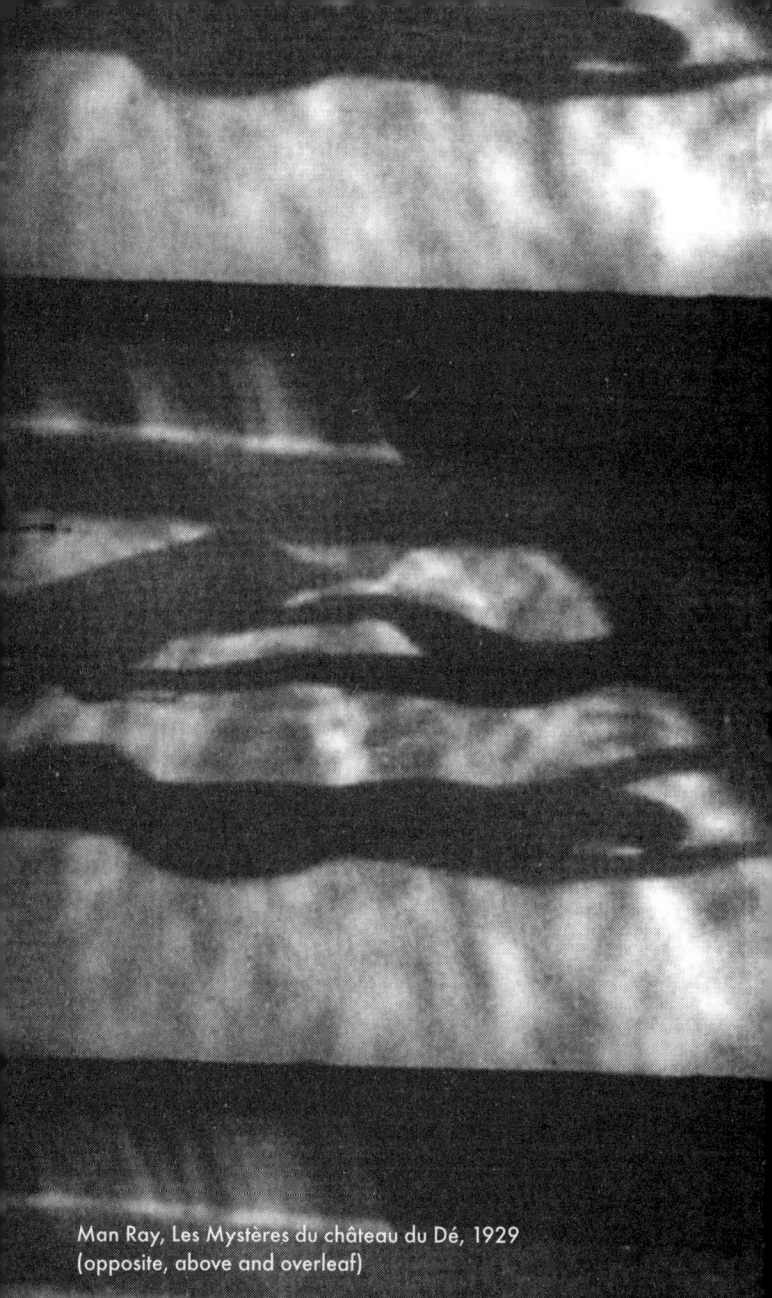

Man Ray, Les Mystères du château du Dé, 1929
(opposite, above and overleaf)

edge of the pool. The fleeting scene of a young woman diving – evidently the model for Aaron's shot – is one of the most memorable moments in the film. Man Ray uses reverse motion, editing the same piece of film twice, running it forwards and backwards, to create the illusion that the diver – in defiance of both reason and gravity – is leaping back towards the stairs she has just jumped from: an experiment in the magic of the medium of film, and a visual palindrome. Man Ray christened this display of cinematic sorcery with a portmanteau of his own invention: 'piscinéma'.

Are Werlemann and Koolhaas trying to do with the Villa dall'Ava what Man Ray did with the Villa Noailles?[68] Might the agent for OMA's licentious, critical distortion of early modernism be the spirit of this other avant-garde that was contemporaneous with, and a rival of, purism – and that Le Corbusier himself was for a brief period vaguely affiliated with? It would not be the first time that Koolhaas had borrowed from surrealism to mock Le Corbusier.

John Guillermin, King Kong, 1976

Let's go back to *S,M,L,XL*, which opens with facsimiles of the beginning and end of *Delirious New York*, as a kind of summary of the prehistory of the author's thinking and career. The presence of 'The Story of the Pool' among the reproduced pages places the Villa dall'Ava, with its pool, in a direct line of descent from the earlier book. In this inaugural work, Koolhaas presents himself as the champion of the 'metropolitan condition', which he postulates was the unconscious invention of American capitalism, appearing first in early twentieth-century Manhattan. He sets out to decipher and retroactively formulate the theory that

Madelon Vriesendorp, Greed, 1973

Franklin J Schaffner, Planet of the Apes, 1968

Salvador Dalí, La Main (les remords de la conscience), 1930

remained implicit in this other modernism, which developed in parallel with the declared architectural avant-gardes, and, in doing so, to renew the very idea of modernity. 'Manhattanism', he writes, 'is a movement which, from all points of view, is the exact opposite of the one we call modern, which is in fact a simple blend of Puritan dogma and repressive good taste'.[69] To prove it, he evokes Le Corbusier's denigration of the vitalist landscape of Manhattan as immature 'child's play … tumult, hairgrowth, first explosive growth of the new middle ages' and his proposal to introduce a little order into this chaos by replacing it with the identical rows of Cartesian skyscrapers of his Radiant City. Now that was something *truly* modern.

Against Le Corbusier's will to power over the tumultuous landscape of Manhattan, Koolhaas opposes (in order to make his own) Salvador Dalí's natural affinity with the delirium of New York, the city the Catalan

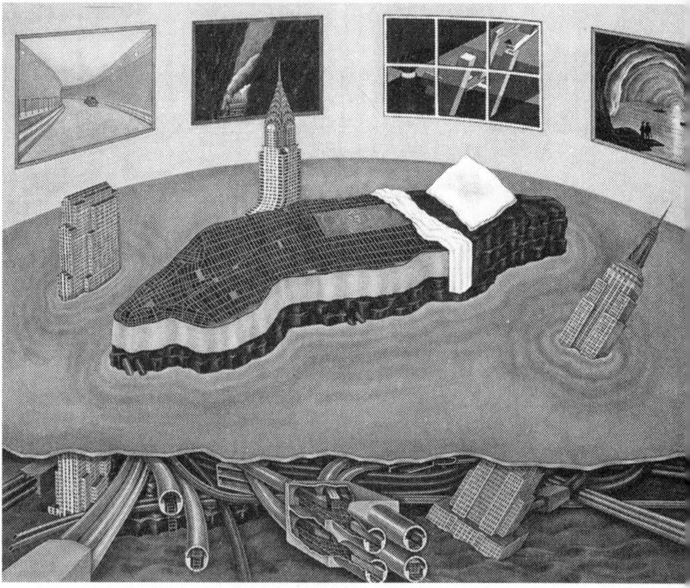

Madelon Vriesendorp, Freud Unlimited, 1975

Postcard, Koolhaas/
Vriesendorp collection, 1940

painter had understood as a manifestation of total surrealism from the moment he set foot in America.[70] A psychoanalysis of Manhattan, *Delirious New York* is impregnated with surrealist motifs, with Koolhaas's declared use of the paranoid-critical method (PCM) – the means Dalí invented of tapping into the unconscious, based on his interpretation of Millet's *Angelus* – mingling with the sources and atmosphere of Vriesendorp's illustrations for the book jacket and the three main chapter heads.[71] It's worth pausing for a moment to consider these images. For too long, they have been seen as mere illustrations of Koolhaas's text, rather than as fragments of a highly personal pictorial work that was created in parallel with the book by an artist who was the author's daily companion. With these works, Vriesendorp uses

the PCM in her own way. André Breton felt that Dalí's invention had given surrealism 'an instrument of primary importance ... capable of being applied with equal success to painting, poetry, the cinema, to the construction of typical surrealist objects, to fashions, to sculpture and even, if necessary, to all manner of exegesis'.[72] Where Dalí mutates the figures of the *Angelus* into anthropomorphic buildings, Vriesendorp goes further, turning the skyscrapers into characters endowed with affects. Her iconic paintings not only embodied the Koolhaasian fiction but helped to feed it, as was made clear a few years ago by the catalogue and exhibition, *The World of Madelon Vriesendorp*.[73] Here, photographs taken by the couple's daughter, Charlie, show the impressive collection of postcards they amassed during their stay in New York to serve as raw material for their work, following in the footsteps of Dalí, who saw them as the 'most vivid documents of modern popular thought' and as natural sources for his painting,[74] but also of Le Corbusier, who treated this mass medium and its representations as both a catalogue of iconographic references and a source of reverie.[75]

Much more than its ideological statements or protocols, it is the *spirit* of surrealism that animates Vriesendorp's paintings. Tapping surrealism's inbuilt propensity to turn any reality into a reservoir of meaningful associations, where images beget more images, her imagination is sparked by the potentially fantastic or grotesque themes that lurk not just in odd postcards but

---

Madelon Vriesendorp, poster for lecture by Rem Koolhaas, New York, 1975

Jean-François Millet, L'Angélus, 1858

OMA, Exodus, or The Voluntary Prisoners of Architecture, 1972

Salvador Dalí, Réminiscence archéologique de l'Angélus de Millet, 1933

Salvador Dalí, New York?, 1938;
Madelon Vriesendorp, Manhattan Angelus, 1975

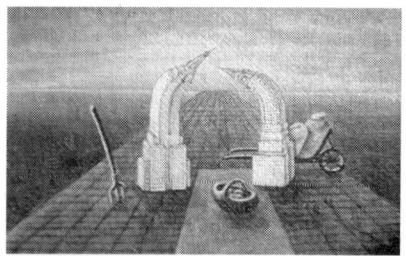

Koolhaas/Vriesendorp postcard collection, 2008

in movie posters, comic strips, knick-knacks, gadgets and indeed all kinds of products of commercial iconography.

Other obsessions of surrealism appear more or less discreetly in Vriesendorp's creations. After the Office for Metropolitan Architecture was founded, she drew an egg hatching a skyscraper as a logo for this newborn, hybrid partnership between two architects and two painters. Its graphic motif mirrors Dali's *Allegory of an American Christmas*, painted by the Catalan artist the same year he and Gala discovered Manhattan. An elusive parable of creation, the egg has long fascinated artists, not least the surrealists; they saw it as a perfect alchemical container where the transmutation of chaotic matter into life is mysteriously performed, out of sight. Even if Vriesendorp's striking logo did not live beyond her initial sketch, eggs appear everywhere in OMA's architectural oeuvre, from the swollen envelope of the Zeebrugge Sea Terminal (1988) to the inflatable balloon of the Serpentine Gallery Pavilion in London

Philippe Halsman, Dali, Mémoire prénatale, 1941

(2006), developed with engineer Cecil Balmond as an eerie incubator for events and talks. The asymmetrical ellipse of the Lille Congrexpo (or better still, Congreggspo) is conceived as an arena where the fertile instability generated by the association of three programmes can exercise itself within a giant, mute precinct, an embodiment of the concept of 'Bigness'.

In S,M,L,XL, a collage gauges its egg-shaped footprint against the 300m height of the Eiffel Tower. 'Cosmic germ of the universe, creation, germ of life, immortality, sun, triad,'[76] reads one of the two 'Egg' entries in the glossary, just before the entry 'Elevator'. With their quotes, they run along the section on an early OMA project, the Netherlands Dance Theatre in The Hague (1981–87, since demolished) whose foyer was graced with a fantastic, quasi-elliptical suspended platform.[77]

Both Koolhaas and Vriesendorp grew up in families of artists whose aesthetic choices took them far from modernism. Surrealism remained influential in the Netherlands in the 1960s, especially in painting,[78] and was still in the air in London, too, when the couple moved there in 1968. As a student at the AA, Koolhaas wrote an essay for Charles Jencks on Dalí and his paranoid-critical

Salvador Dalí, Allégorie d'un Noël américain, 1934

method. *The Angelus* appears in collages from the beginning of OMA: in the manner of Dalí, Millet's peasants are relocated, diverted in this case into the prison setting of one of the scenes in *Exodus* (1972).[79] And the Millet painting, or rather one of Dalí's reworkings of it, appears again, on top of one of the granite

plinths of *The City of the Captive Globe*, symbolising the paranoid-critical method. After this, the reference expands into two of Vriesendorp's most celebrated paintings: the unforgettable scenes of *Flagrant Délit* and *Après l'Amour*, with their enchanted skyscrapers turning towards each other in bed. This motif is taken up in order to push further Dalí's reinterpretations of ruins and skyscrapers in his reworking of *The Angelus* (*Architectonic Angelus* and *New York!*), which were themselves the result of the Catalan surrealist's earlier hijacking of Millet's peasants. While he was working on *Delirious New York* – a Dalínian title if ever there was one – Koolhaas gave a number of lectures on 'Dalí & Le

---

Madelon Vriesendorp, draft design for OMA logo, 1975 (above); (overleaf, top to bottom, left to right) Max Ernst, La Femme 100 têtes, Suite B, 1929; Detail from Pieter Bruegel the Elder, Patientia, 1561; Salvador Dalí, Enfant géopolitique observant la naissance de l'homme nouveau, 1943; Christian (Georges Herbiet), L'Oeuf pourri, 1921

Corbusier: The Paranoid-Critical Method', a topic that clearly absorbed him at the time.[80] In 1978, the same year *Delirious New York* appeared, *AD* magazine published a special issue on architecture and surrealism guest-edited by AA unit master Dalibor Veseley. The cover image was Dalí's *Architectonic Angelus*, and Koolhaas's book chapter on Dalí and Le Corbusier featured prominently.[81]

Thus, taking his cue from Dalí's treatment of *The Angelus* – Millet's best-known work and one of the most popular paintings in the history of art – Koolhaas would, with the Villa dall'Ava, deform the Villa Savoye – Le Corbusier's most celebrated building and one of the most emblematic works of the purist movement. An inspiration for *Delirious New York* and its iconography and, more broadly, a wellspring of Koolhaas's thinking at the time, does Dalí play a role in the architecture of Villa dall'Ava? And if so, what is it?

Madelon Vriesendorp, Flagrant Délit, 1975

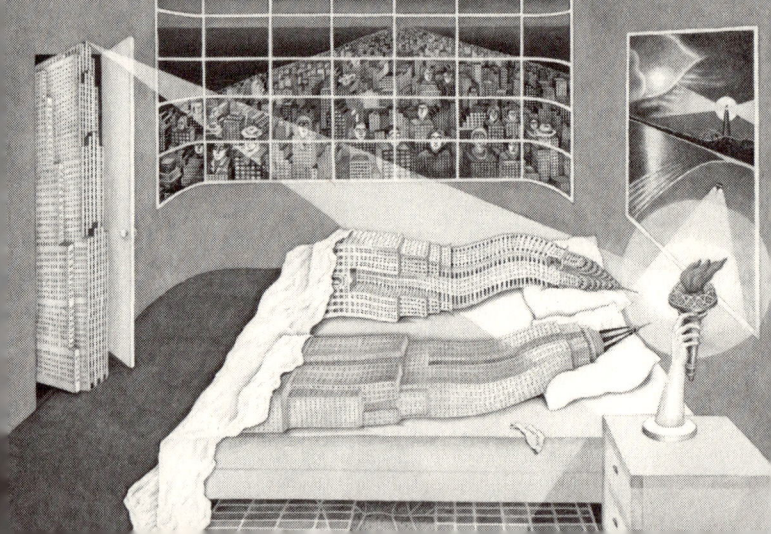

AVIDALL'AVA

Let's go back to the series of photographs in *S,M,L,XL*, and specifically to the zaniest, most inexplicable plate of all: the view looking down the ramp – that is to say, in the direction of Paris – where we glimpse off to the left, behind the glazed facade, an unidentified person leading a giraffe down the driveway. Along with others extracted from the same sequence, this image created quite a stir beyond the pages of *S,M,L,XL* (at times overshadowing all the rest, to Werlemann's regret).[82] Which makes the near-silence of almost every single architectural critic on the subject quite intriguing, like one of those set pieces in a classic comedy film: important people doing everything in their power to ignore the ministrations of an embarrassing intruder in their midst.[83] So what could

Romeo the giraffe inside the front gate, 1991

be the meaning of this giraffe that is apparently so hard to see? Is the introduction of this scene into *S,M,L,XL* part of Koolhaas's strategy of one-upmanship over Le Corbusier? Because the appearance of an African herbivore in a pretty coat may be – as Roberto Gargiani has suggested – a response to a 1930 painting by the English surrealist Christopher Wood depicting a zebra posing on the terrace of the Villa Savoye.[84] In the same vein, Koolhaas seems to want to trigger a poetic reaction with this meeting of opposites – wild animal and rational dwelling, primitivism and machinism. This importing of a beautiful flesh-and-blood beast into a modern villa may also – on the contrary, and with all the irony that this implies – hark back to the sinister still-*death* with a fish assembled in the kitchen of the villa at Garches and photographed for *L'Architecture vivante* in 1929.

Christopher Wood, Zebra and Parachute, 1930

Elephants from the Hagenbeck circus outside Le Corbusier's Maison Blanche, 1914

Robert Doisneau, Le Corbusier with his Dog Pinceau, 1944

Kitchen at the Villa Stein, L'Architecture vivante, 1929

Lucian Freud, The Painter's Room, 1944

Le Corbusier and Charles de Beistegui, roof terrace at the Beistegui penthouse, 1929 (above and opposite)

Or to the one project by Le Corbusier that historians file under the rubric of surrealism, the rooftop terrace of the Beistegui apartment, where a parrot – actually an automaton perched on a Murano glass pole – presides over the baroque furnishings of an open-air 'living room'. A sketch by Le Corbusier of this salon *en plein air* shows Paris reduced to its two most famous monuments, the Arc de Triomphe and the Eiffel Tower, which rise as a pair above the railings of the terrace. Although their pairing is in fact impossible from this vantage point, these two 'surrealised' emblems constitute the view, to the exclusion of the rest of the city.

This allusion could also point in the direction of a surrealism *avant la lettre* that has, since Hieronymus Bosch, animated a whole facet of Flemish

Le Corbusier, roof terrace, Beistegui penthouse, 1928

OMA sketch collage of the rooftop terrace, Villa dall'Ava, 1985

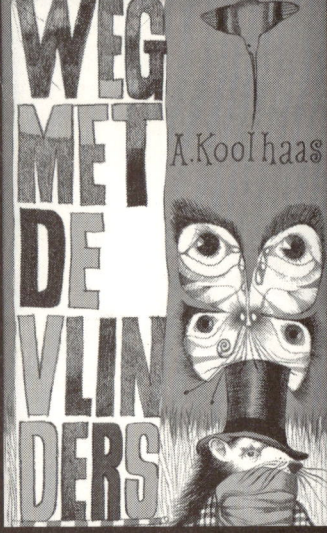

artistic culture, and in which animals, familiar or fantastic, occupy a place of choice. An offshoot of this tradition was very much part of Koolhaas's childhood. His father Anton (1912–1992), an acknowledged expert on wildlife who scripted documentaries on the subject, is famous in the Netherlands for his surreal animal novellas, which have largely remained untranslated and are therefore little known outside the Dutch-speaking world.[85] A spider, an ant, a sparrow and a bat are among the minuscule heroes of these tales, which 'are part of a long tradition, but ... unlike anything else in the genre. These are not fairytales or parables, since although rich in symbolism they often exhibit an acute despair and a cool determination that belong to modern realist literature.'[86] The covers of the original editions are sometimes illustrated with animals dressed in clothes, like characters subject to the same dilemmas as humans, in a sort of continuation of the project of French fabulist and moralist Jean de La Fontaine. Werlemann has said that he had planned to use other animals as props for the shoot at the Villa dall'Ava – among them a black panther and a large snake – but in the end had to make do with Romeo, a young giraffe borrowed from a nearby zoo.[87] The filmmaker justifies its presence by referring to a tale by the Dutch writer Frans Kellendonk (who had died shortly before) that celebrated the giraffe, beautiful and silent, at once enormous and light, 'pliable and transportable like a tripod', walking down the street and stopping to 'look inside me'.[88]

Anton Koolhaas, De hond in het lege huis, 1964; Gekke Witte, 1959; Vleugels voor een Rat, 1967; Weg met de vlinders, 1961

The giraffe has long held a special place in the teeming zoo of art, its representation inextricably linked to a perennial fascination with the deviant and the bizarre. From the time of its discovery, and even more since its arrival in Europe, this animal with a long neck, strange proportions and asymmetrical legs, the head of a ruminant and the coat of a wild cat, has been an enduring source of fascination for scholars, artists and the population at large. Its species name, *Giraffa camelopardalis* (camel-marked-like-a-leopard), describes a chimerical creature, an aberration, an overturning of nature's order. Bosch painted a giraffe alongside an elephant and

Romeo the giraffe at the Villa dall'Ava, 1991 (below, opposite and overleaf)

a unicorn in the *Eden* panel of his *Garden of Earthly Delights* (1503–04). Along with other exotic animals, it then found its way into Italian mannerism via the grotesque decorations created by Giulio Romano in the Vatican in 1516.[89] Grotesques had become fashionable with the rediscovery of the subterranean spaces of the Domus Aurea at the end of the previous century: the decorations of Nero's former home, featuring prodigious animals and monstrous hybrids, upturned the idea of ancient representation, infusing it with an element of the fantastical and the whimsical. Something of the medieval sense of mystery and enchantment attached

Giraffe from Bianco Noe, Viaggio da Venetia al Santo Sepolcro, 1600 (top); Adrian Collaert, Animalium Quadrupedum, 1633 (above); Hieronymus Bosch, The Garden of Delights, 1504 (opposite)

Giraffe engraving, Italy, 1525

Giovanni Da Udine, Grotesque Frescoes, 1519

Abraham De Bruyn, Landscape with Various Animals and other Creatures, 1578

to these creatures lingered for a long time on the margins of the modern era, and would be captured and exploited by the surrealists. Beasts populate the childlike, magical worlds of jungles and idols conjured by Douanier Rousseau and Frida Kahlo. From Max Ernst to Leonora Carrington, the visual productions of the surrealists abound with a multitude of animals, just like the popular illustrations that inspired them, such as John Tenniel's engravings for *Alice's in Wonderland* or JJ Grandville's extraordinary social caricatures. The arrival of the first giraffe in Paris in 1827 created a mania for all things giraffe-themed. Grandville, too, had a particular fondness for this animal.

JJ Grandville, Scènes de la vie privée et publique des animaux, 1842

Carel Willink, Giraffen in het park van Versailles, 1956

In the Netherlands in the 1950s and 1960s, a number of leading artists continued to depict animals in a surrealist or fantastic vein. The virtuoso illustrator Peter Vos (1935–2010) made animals – the lion, birds – his main subject, viewed from a social perspective that links him to Grandville; Vos also illustrated the covers of some of Anton Koolhaas's books. Carel Willink (1900–1983) painted a series of canvases showing large African herbivores wandering around famous classical French gardens, including one of a pair of giraffes stationed at the foot of the Orangerie staircase at Versailles (*Giraffen in het park van Versailles*, 1956). Willink developed a style of magic realism derived from the metaphysical paintings of Giorgio de Chirico, composing imaginary

scenes and landscapes from existing elements documented by photography: so many montages of true facts – faces, buildings, ruins, panoramas, animals – pressed into the service of alternative visual realities. Naturally, the glossary of S,M,L,XL contains an entry on 'Animals', in which Koolhaas quotes an extract from Demetri Porphyrios quoting Foucault quoting Borges quoting the famous taxonomy of animals in a Chinese encyclopedia.[90]

A further allusion to the rhizome-like propagation of stories, myths, references and their meanings through the infinite circulation of texts in time and history?

But more than anything else, the giraffe is one of the fetish animals in the Dalí bestiary. You don't have to look for long at his paintings, drawings, or installations before a specimen wanders into the scene, its mane in flames. With its phallic neck, the burning giraffe represented 'the masculine cosmic apocalyptic monster', Dalí proclaimed in his essay, 'The Terrifying and Edible Beauty of Art Nouveau Architecture', in which he held forth about his loathing of rationalist modernism and his love

---

Salvador Dalí, Vénus à la girafe, 1973 (above); Salvador Dalí, Girafe en feu, 1936 (opposite)

for Gaudí and art nouveau (and from which Koolhaas drew the title of one of his most powerful texts of the 1980s).[91] Riffing on the imagination of Bosch, Dalí modifies the anatomy of other animals to conform with that of the giraffe: for example, in his *Temptation of St Anthony*

Pierre Patte, after Charles-François Ribart de Chamoust, Architecture singulière, l'éléphant triomphal, grand kiosque à la gloire du Roi, 1758

– a subject well suited to the visual expression of all manner of delusions, treated by Bosch in his time, along many others, and also adapted by Méliès in the early days of cinema – where he gives a horse and elephants spidery legs and has them carry heavy burdens on their backs.

Werlemann thus summons an animal laden with intense symbolism to the Villa dall'Ava, immortalising this improbable encounter in a photograph that Koolhaas chooses to present in the pages of *S,M,L,XL*. Gargiani sees in Koolhaas's visual quotation of the giraffe an analogy with the inversion of gravity staged in the villa: the 40-tonne mass of the swimming pool seemingly carried by the thin and indecisive pilotis.[92] Extrapolating from there, a doubly surrealist intention might be discerned in the photograph in *S,M,L,XL*. In confronting the villa with a real-life giraffe – a naturally mannerist animal, a living anamorphosis – and capturing this encounter on film, Koolhaas is deploying a device suggested by surrealism, and more specifically by Dalí, to trigger and then fix an association between several elements of his project that up to then had remained latent. Most obviously, there are the slender stilts that raise the heavy living quarters as if by magic. But added to this, there is the pattern of the *opus incertum* – brown with light mortar – that clads the base of the villa (the stone, cold and mineral, evokes by antiphrasis the warm and sensual skin of the giraffe, and underscores the artificiality of the building). And then there is the resonance of both of these metaphors with the symbol of the capital: the distant silhouette of the Eiffel Tower,[93] an iron giraffe on crutches, a rational enterprise (by an engineer) taken to the point of

irrationality (its lack of obvious function), whose ritual immolation, every 14 July, transforms its abstract structure into an animal of fire. The many recurrences of the association between the Eiffel Tower and a giraffe in popular representations only reinforce this interpretation. Frans Kellendonk, too, saw in this animal the 'Eiffel Tower of the animal kingdom'.[94]

Should we also understand the presence of the giraffe as a conceptual allegory, an underhand affirmation of Koolhaas's earlier stance on architecture? Irina Davidovici detects in sections of *Delirious New York* 'a similitude to the mannerists ... where Koolhaas turns away from the given reality to search the essence

---

Anonymous, Paris Métamorphoses, undated

of architecture within himself, inspired by Salvador Dalí's method of "propping" the soft amorphous mass of the unconscious with the rigid "crutch" of Cartesian rationality'.[95] With its drawer/pool supported by a sort of tuning fork, Dalí's *Venus à la giraffe* sculpture (1973) is a fairly straightforward representation of this, and could almost pass for an early conceptual model of the Villa dall'Ava. In introducing a real-life giraffe to spice up his account of the house, Koolhaas sets up a riddle with multiple strands suggesting different interpretations of his project – all of which come together to point to Dalínian surrealism as the agent behind this transformation of the rigorist *machine à habiter* into a theatre of delirium, of the Apollonian into the Dionysian. Like Dalí, whose elephants metamorphose into spiders, in the image of

Eiffel Tower postcard, 1925

Eiffel Tower, Bastille Day, 1990

his fetish animal, Koolhaas ironically fleshes out the anatomical fable that Le Corbusier deployed to denigrate the skyscrapers of Manhattan: 'Imagine a man undergoing a mysterious disturbance of his organic life; the torso remains normal, but his legs become ten or twenty times too long.'[96] In this light, the inlaying of a Vermeer painting into the villa's litigious facade acquires an additional meaning: that of a salute to Dalí, who, as we know, identified with the Flemish painter in an obsessive manner.

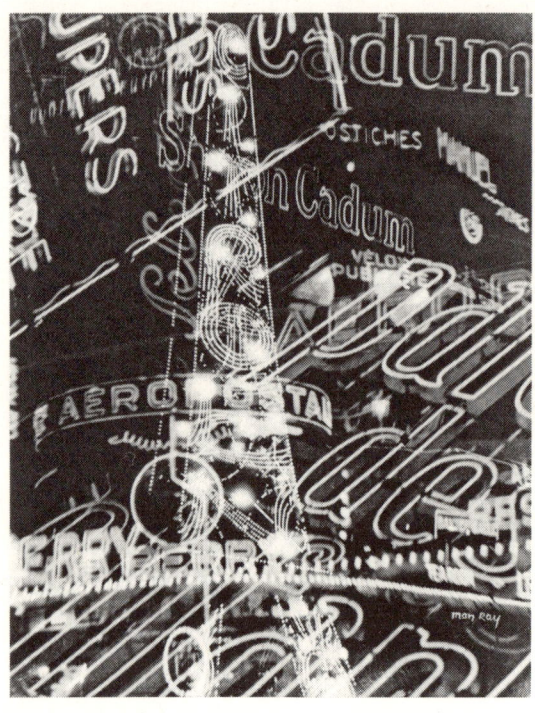

Man Ray, La Ville (Electricité), 1931 (above); Charles Cordat, La Tour Eiffel, preface by Le Corbusier, 1955 (opposite)

LA TOUR EIFFEL

Préface de LE CORBUSIER

LES GRANDES RÉUSSITES FRANÇAISES

There is, moreover, a famous precedent for the idea of fomenting a retroactive plot by means of a covert surrealist operation. In his unforgettable study of Jean-Jacques Lequeu, historian Philippe Duboÿ attributes similar motives to Marcel Duchamp, whom he tells us spent a considerable amount of time in the archives of the Bibliothèque Nationale tampering with some plates by the architect-draftsman, who was like him a native of Rouen.[97] Duboÿ's book, subtitled 'An Architectural Enigma', pieces together the fragments of an enquiry as detailed as it is paranoiac; the English edition was published in 1986, that is, at the very moment when OMA was finalising the project for the Villa dall'Ava. The unclassifiable work of that

Jean-Jacques Lequeu, frontispiece, Nouvelle méthode appliquée, 1792

eroto-graphomaniac had previously been associated with Ledoux and Boullée, as part of Emil Kaufmann's troika of 'revolutionary architects' who anticipated the modern movement.[98] Thirty-five years later, Duboÿ's rediscovery and exhibition of this delirious iconography would trigger alternative interpretations of Lequeu: on the one hand, a virtuoso exponent of architectural parody for the purposes of subversion (by means of design, 'he succeeded in satirising and throwing into question all the sacred conventions of the academy and fashion alike',[99] proposes Anthony Vidler, and Koolhaas might well be following in his footsteps here); or, on the other hand, a precursor of Robert Venturi and postmodernism.

Man Ray, La ville, 1931

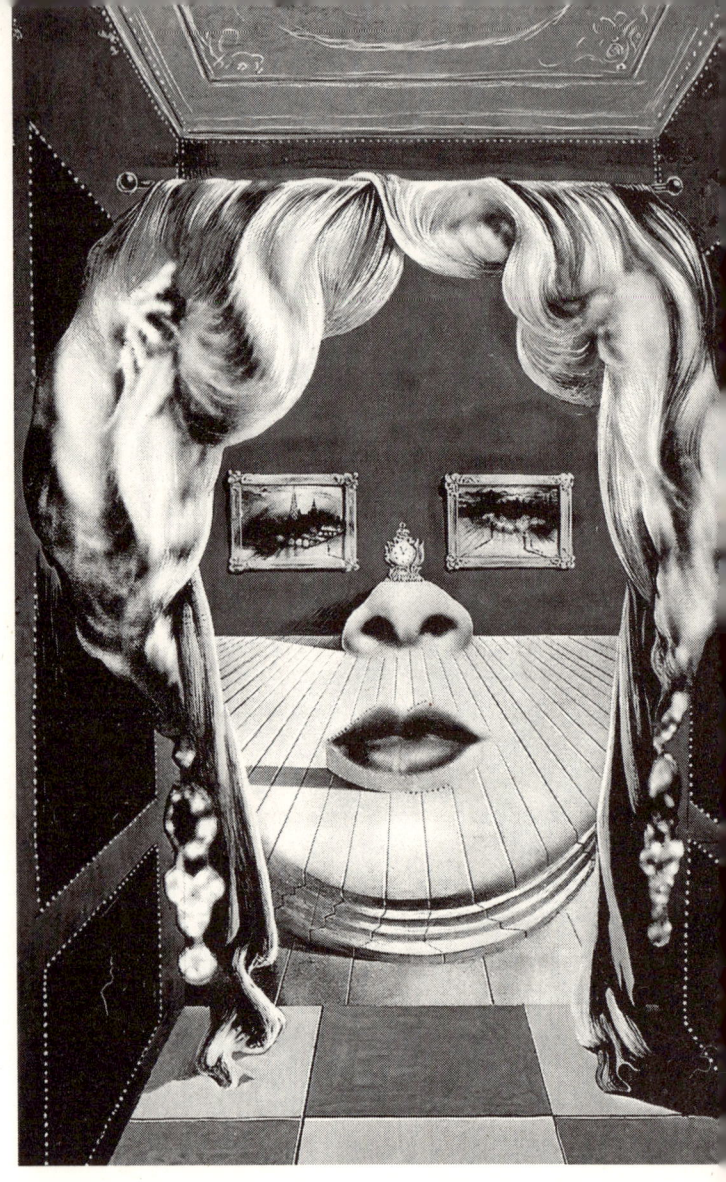

Salvador Dalí, Visage de Mae West (pouvant être utilisé comme appartement surréaliste), 1934 (above); Madelon Vriesendorp, Sketch for Dalíing Around (Portrait of Rem Koolhaas), 1991 (opposite)

EYES WIDE SHUT

Now we've got to this point, let's sum up our charade. The Villa dall'Ava, the perverted twin of Le Corbusier's purist houses, is a built critique, a materialisation of the delirious potential of modernism, the outcome of an underhand operation directed by the corrosive forces of functionalism's best enemy within the avant-garde – Dalí's radical surrealism. It's also Koolhaas's *casa come me*, his cultural self-portrait at that stage of his career, which by extension embodies his project for architecture in the period immediately after *Delirious New York*. This last hypothesis is supported by a Vriesendorp sketch dated the year of the villa's completion: a portrait of Koolhaas, humorously titled *Sketch for Dalíing Around*, in which the architect's face overlaps with architectural elements of the villa. This drawing is an explicit corollary to Dalí's *Mae West's Face Which May Be Used as a Surrealist Apartment* (1934) and to an earlier paraphrase of that work: the bedroom Carlo Mollino designed for the Casa Devalle in Turin, with its curtains and lips sofa (1939).[100]

The Villa dall'Ava contains many other shared themes and connections between Dalí and Koolhaas: a taste for exposing the body to danger, for making a spectacle of the touch of evil that lurks behind every good intention and a cold manipulation of its most disturbing aspects, a defiant aversion to intangible moral truths. In 1929, Dalí and Luis Buñuel made a film that condensed all these obsessions, the surrealist film par excellence, *Un chien andalou*. In its famous – unbearable – opening scene, a man stands in front of a window, slowly sharpening a razor and then, seeing a thin cloud passing over the moon, slices through the eye of the woman sitting next to him. This act of wanton cruelty, synonymous with absolute horror – psychoanalysis has shown that the fear of losing our sight is one of the most deep-rooted of human terrors – is triggered by the association between the white orb of the moon and the globe of the eye on the one hand and the blade and the cloud on the other. The close-up of

---

Luis Buñuel and Salvador Dalí, Un chien andalou, 1929

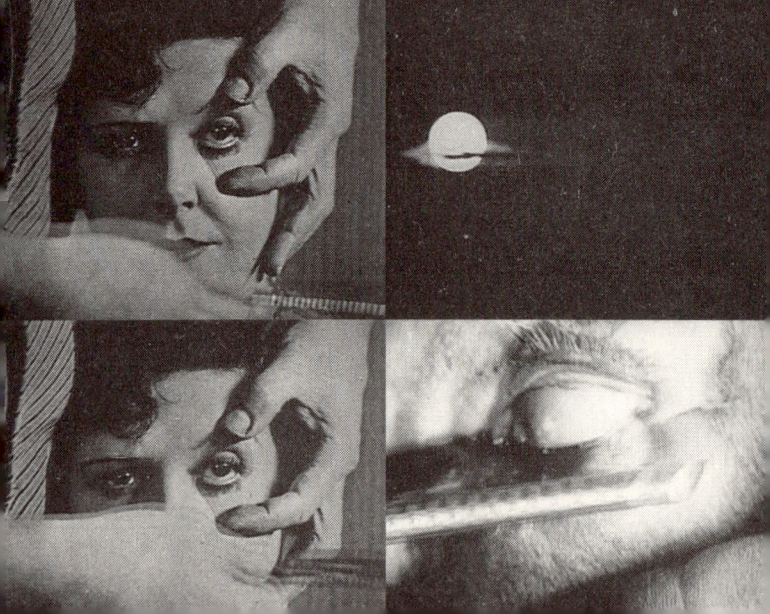

Carlo Mollino, Casa Devalle, 1940

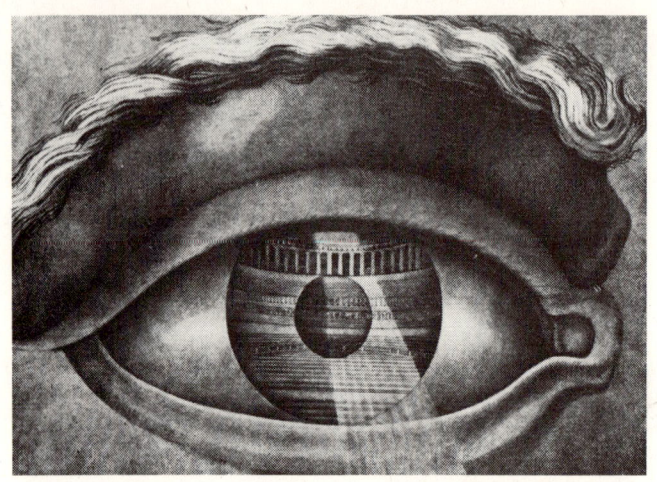

Claude-Nicolas Ledoux, Œil reflétant l'intérieur du théâtre de Besançon, 1804

Dalí and Buñuel's sliced eye has been seen as inversely related to Claude-Nicolas Ledoux's *The Interior of the Theatre at Besançon Reflected in the Pupil of an Eye* (1804), and thus interpreted – notably by Juhani Pallasmaa – as a critical parable of the 'oculocentrism' of western modernity.[101] But Koolhaas has a more pessimistic reading of this famous scene that is certainly more in tune with the intentions of the two surrealists, one that focuses on its destabilising of the good, the equivocal pleasure that emerges from it and the imaginary potential it conceals. Koolhaas would choose a pair of these terror-freighted images to illustrate two of his early works in *S,M,L,XL*: 'The Berlin Wall as Architecture', done while he was a student at the AA in 1972, and the OMA project for the renovation of the panopticon prison in Arnhem (1980). Both can be seen as

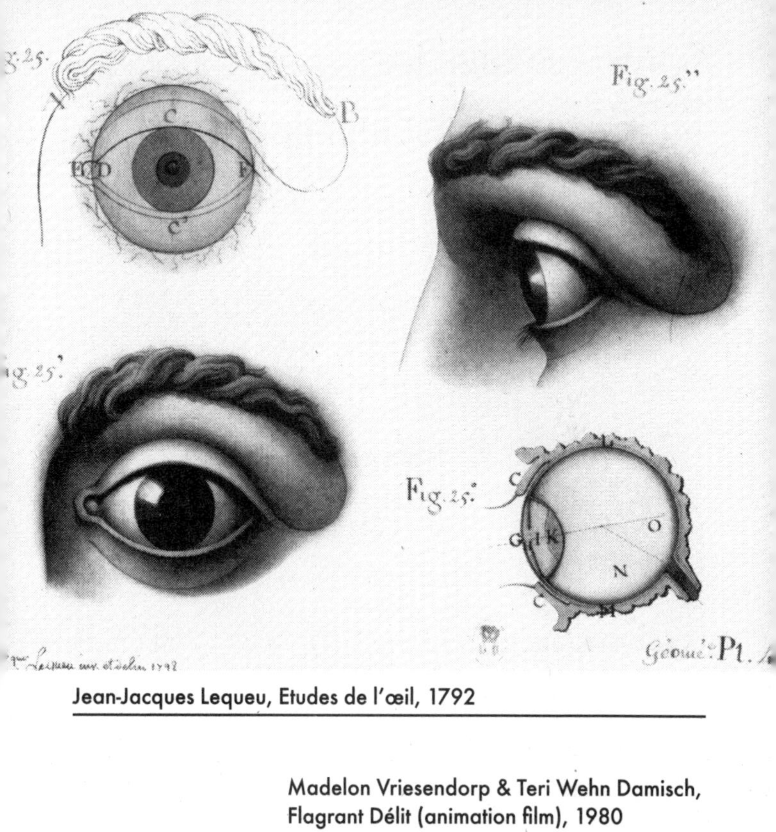

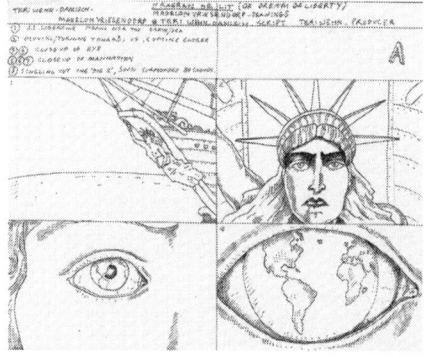

Jean-Jacques Lequeu, Etudes de l'œil, 1792

Madelon Vriesendorp & Teri Wehn Damisch,
Flagrant Délit (animation film), 1980

incandescent reflections on the power of architecture to confine and surveil,[102] or as a reaction to the innocent belief in its capacity to improve lives, as he said of his dystopia *Exodus, or the Voluntary Prisoners of Architecture* (1972), whose fictional scenario, based on

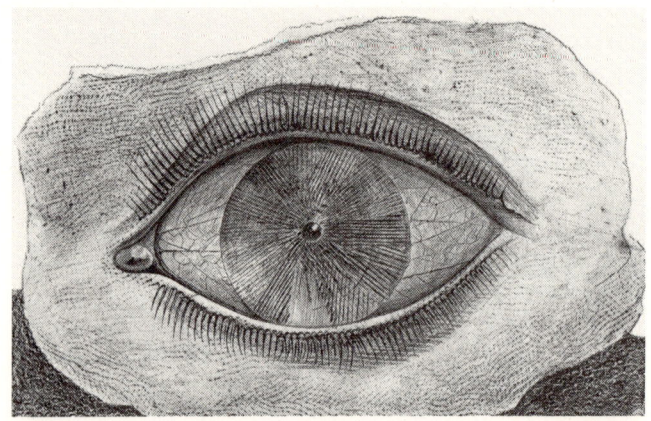

Max Ernst, La Roue de la lumière, 1926 (top); René Magritte, Le faux miroir, 1929 (above)

André Masson, frontispiece for Georges Bataille,
Histoire de l'œil, 1928

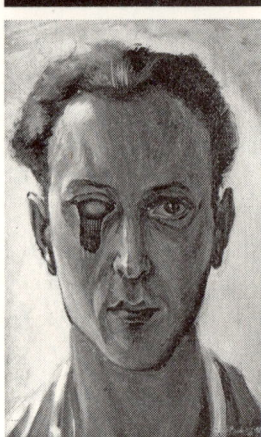

the Berlin Wall study, played with precisely these themes.

But is this repellent act of sight deprivation also the one that *opens*, quite literally, the eyes? Dalí's and Koolhaas's intersecting allusions to this ambiguous and morbid spectacle call to mind the curses uttered by Le Corbusier, the slayer of 'eyes which do not see'.[103] Le Corbusier, who could only see with one eye, held vision to be the supreme faculty, while the eye was a major obsession of surrealism. From Max Ernst to Man Ray, from the draftsmen who preceded them – Lequeu and Grandville – to Magritte and of course Dalí, all made spectacular use of this organ, representing it in innumerable ways. Unsurprisingly, the word 'Eyes' is the subject of three entries in the *S,M,L,XL* glossary. The first is illustrated by a quote from Le Corbusier, the anathema hammered out in *Toward an Architecture*, the second by a Proustian aphorism about how a real voyage of discovery consists not in seeing new

---

André Breton, photobooth self-portrait, 1924 (top); Victor Brauner, self-portrait, 1931 (above)

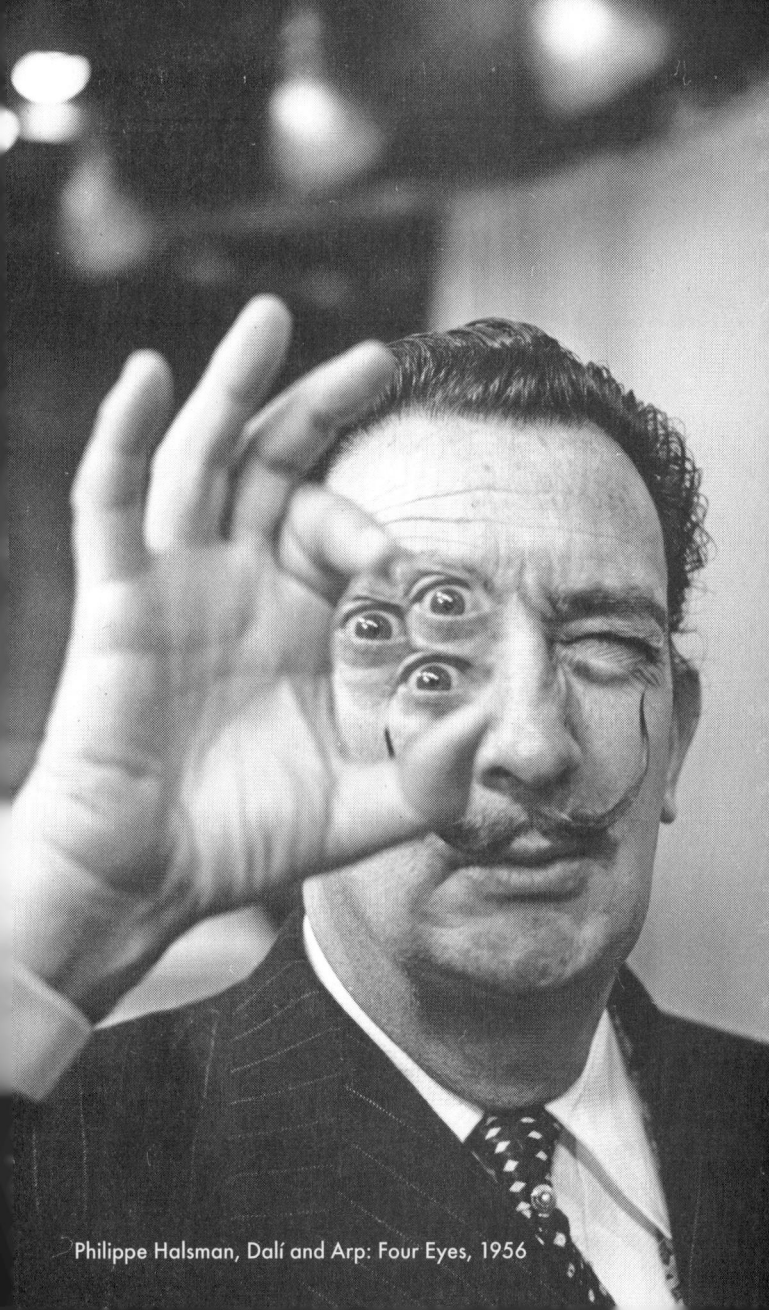

Philippe Halsman, Dalí and Arp: Four Eyes, 1956

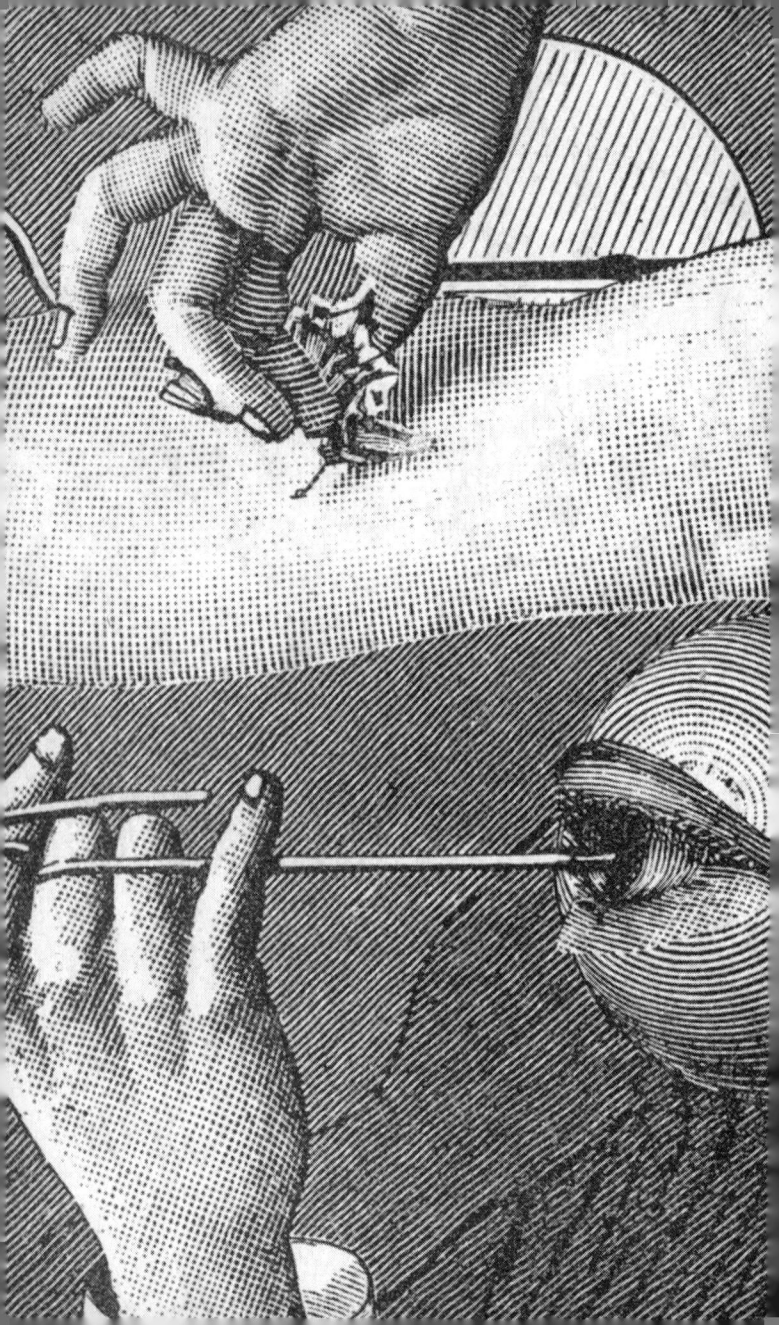

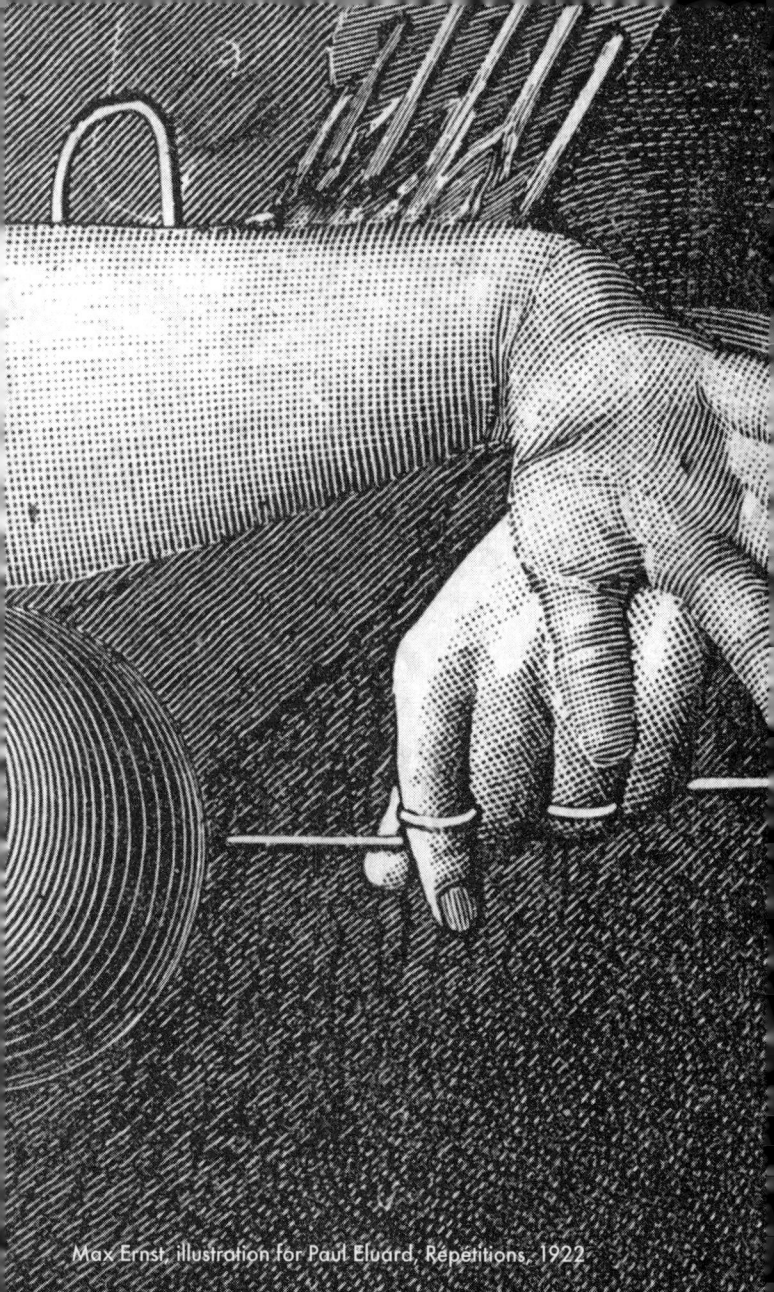

Max Ernst, illustration for Paul Eluard, Répétitions, 1922

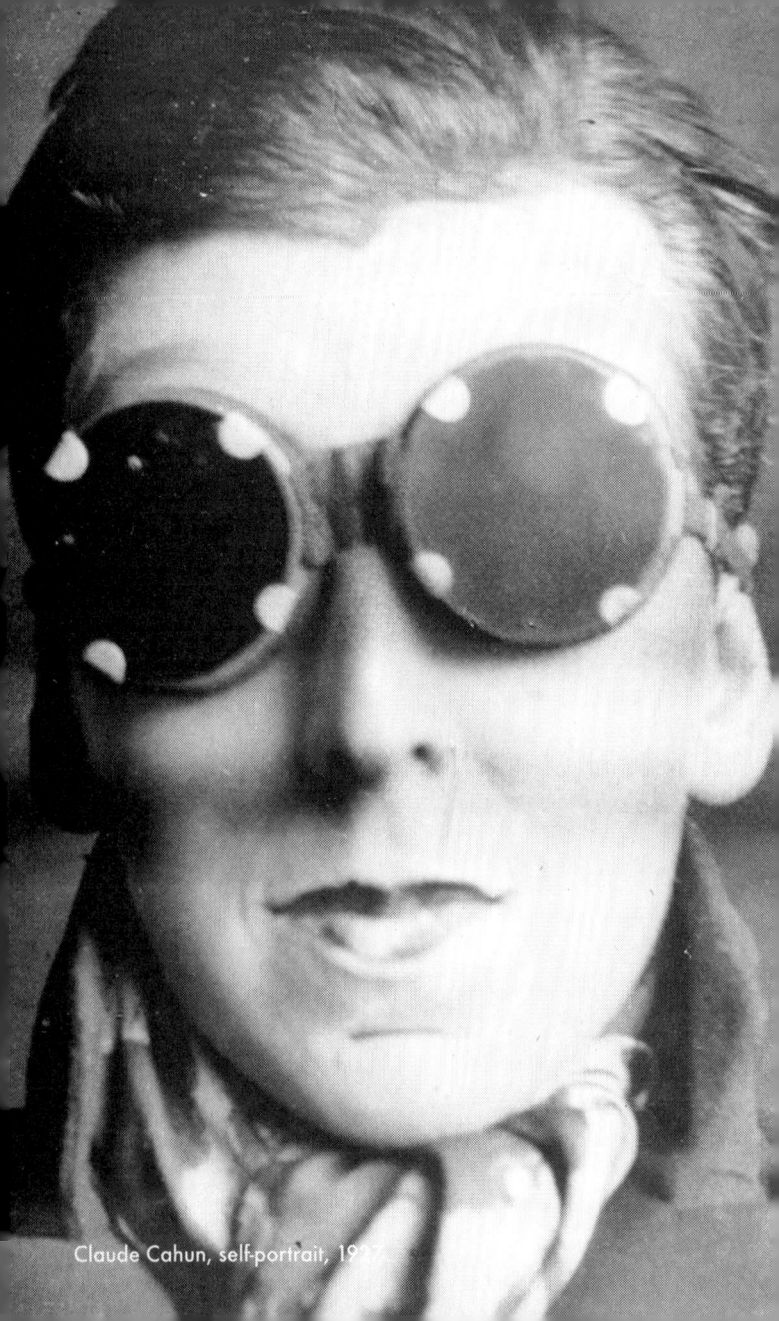

Claude Cahun, self-portrait, 1927

Piero Martina, Carlo Mollino Flying Over Manhattan, 1942

sights but in looking with new eyes and the third by an eye-gouging scene taken from Jerzy Kosinski's novel, *The Painted Bird* (1965).[104] Then, as F naturally follows E, these three versions of the word 'Eyes' seamlessly give way to a definition of the word 'Facade', this time from Koolhaas, who uses it to point out once more that the supposedly 'heroic' condition of the architect is but a superficial illusion.[105]

Orchestrated under the guise of alphabetical logic, Koolhaas's deliberate bringing together of the two terms makes one think, funnily enough, of a late Dalí collage, *Architecture of the Eyes* (1970), where the Catalan painter extrapolates to the point of absurdity the conception of the facade – the well-known analogy with the face, with the openings being eyes – that has prevailed since the Renaissance.[106] With a soft facade juxtaposing 27 identical eyes, arranged as a stack of fixed gazes in a uniform grid, like industrial panels, Dalí ridicules both the anthropomorphic pretensions of classicism *and* the iconographic poverty of modernism, giving us instead an unsettling decor of ambiguous monumentality.

This further connection between Koolhaas and Dalí acquires a tinge of bitter irony in light of the fact that the lawsuit filed by the neighbours of the Villa dall'Ava was based not so much on aesthetic objections as on their fear that their privacy would be violated by the large glazed surfaces of the side elevation. After several years of litigation, it took a decision by the Conseil d'État to settle the question of whether a glass wall really was a wall – the legal version of a well-worn modernist quarrel, in short. It was thus a trivial matter of *vis-à-vis* (literally, face to face) and right to view that forced Koolhaas

Salvador Dalí, Projet d'architecture, 1976

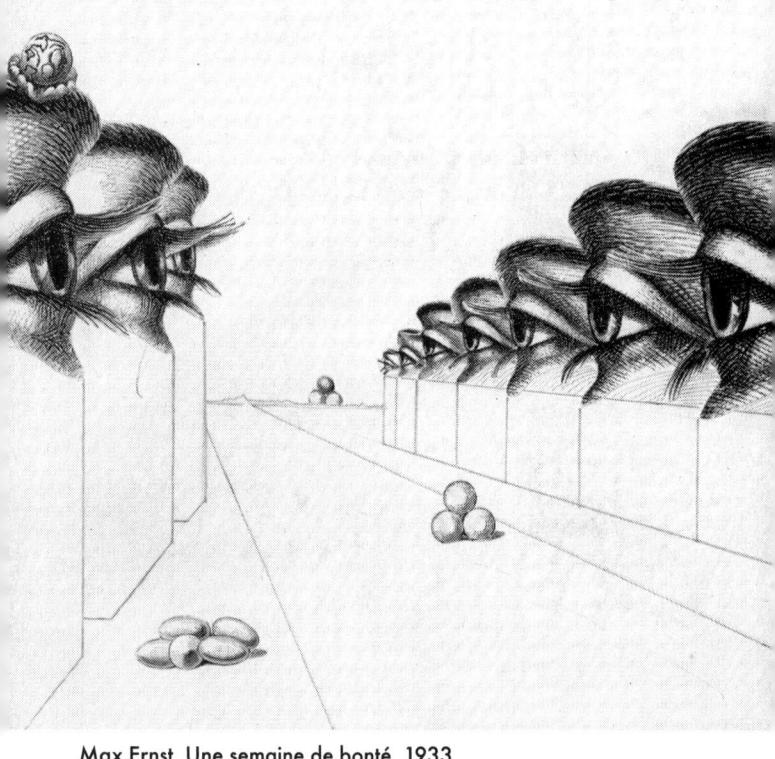

Max Ernst, Une semaine de bonté, 1933

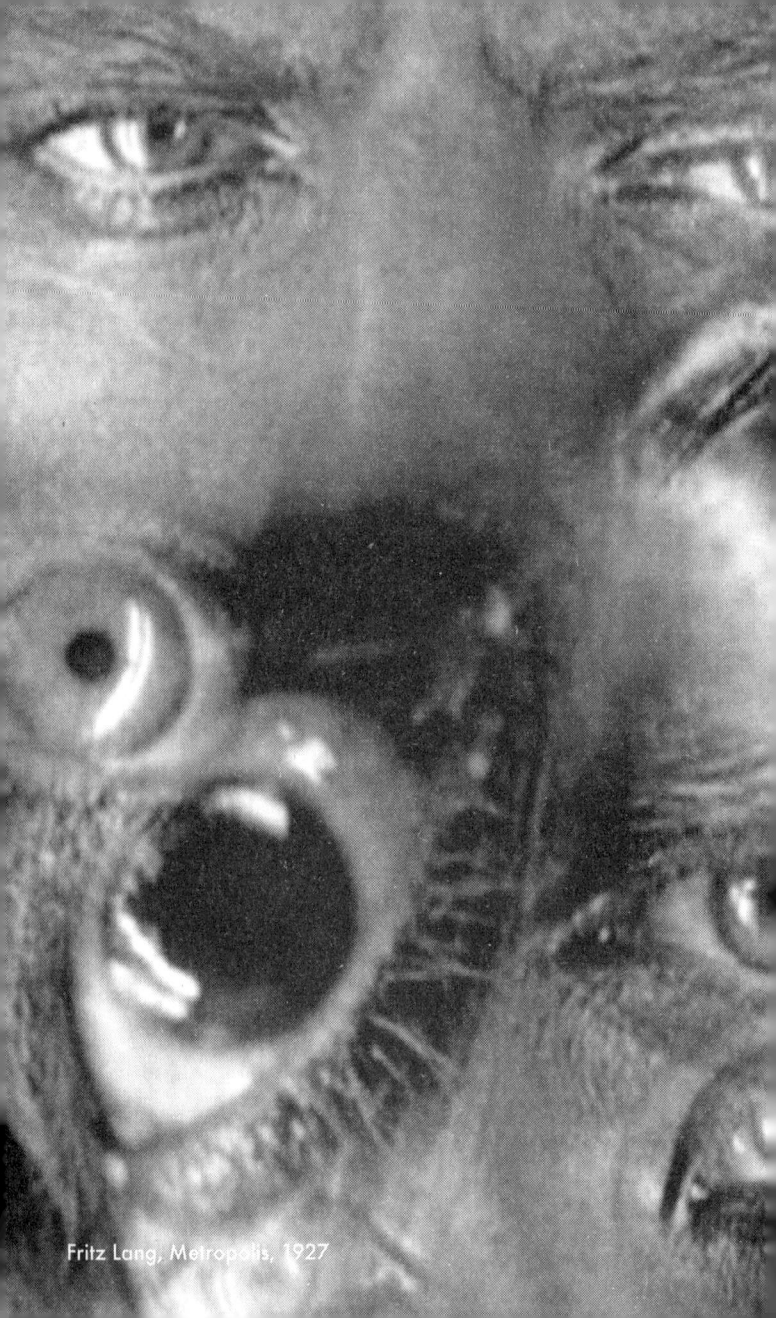

Fritz Lang, Metropolis, 1927

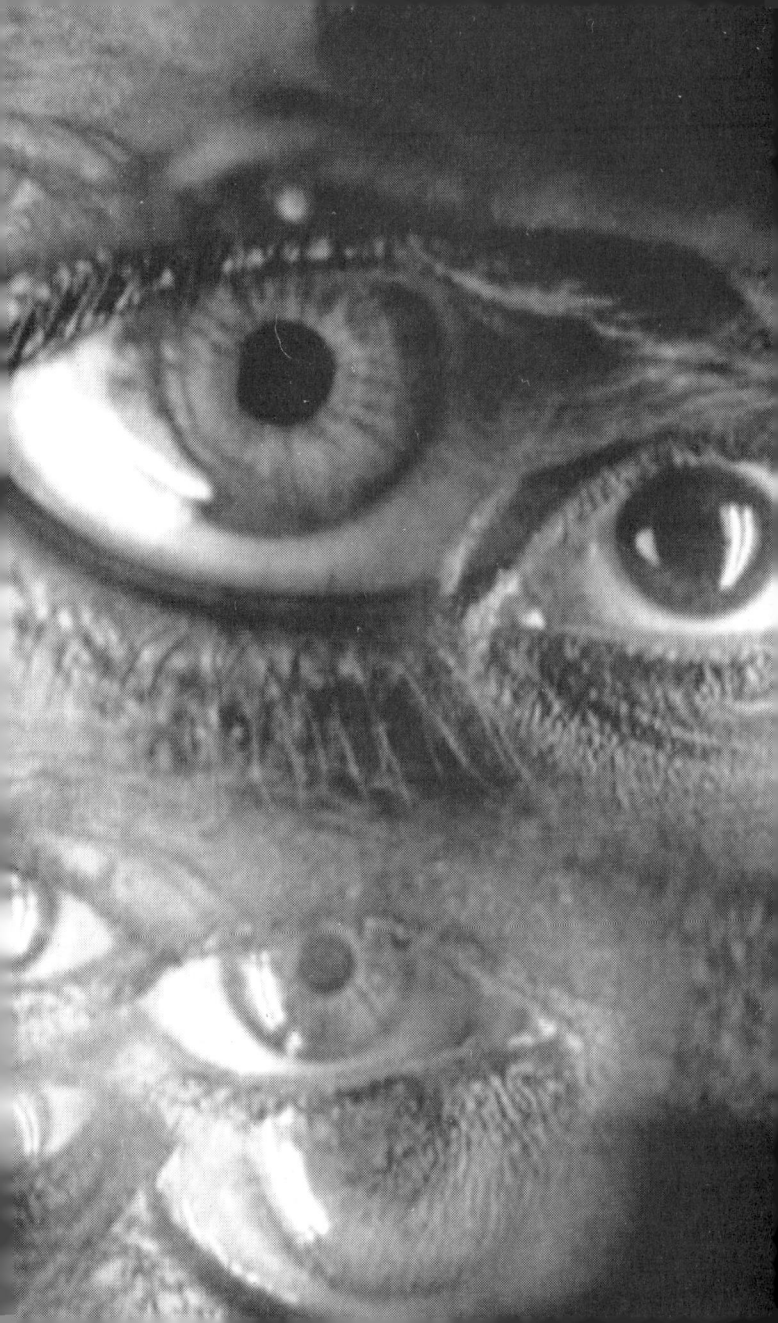

Russian poster, Dziga Vertov, Man with a Movie Camera, 1929

Aleksandr Rodchenko, KinoGlatz, 1924

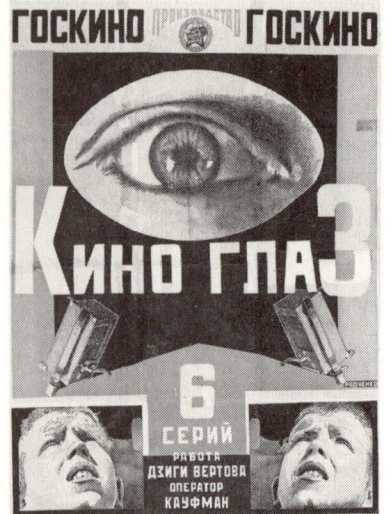

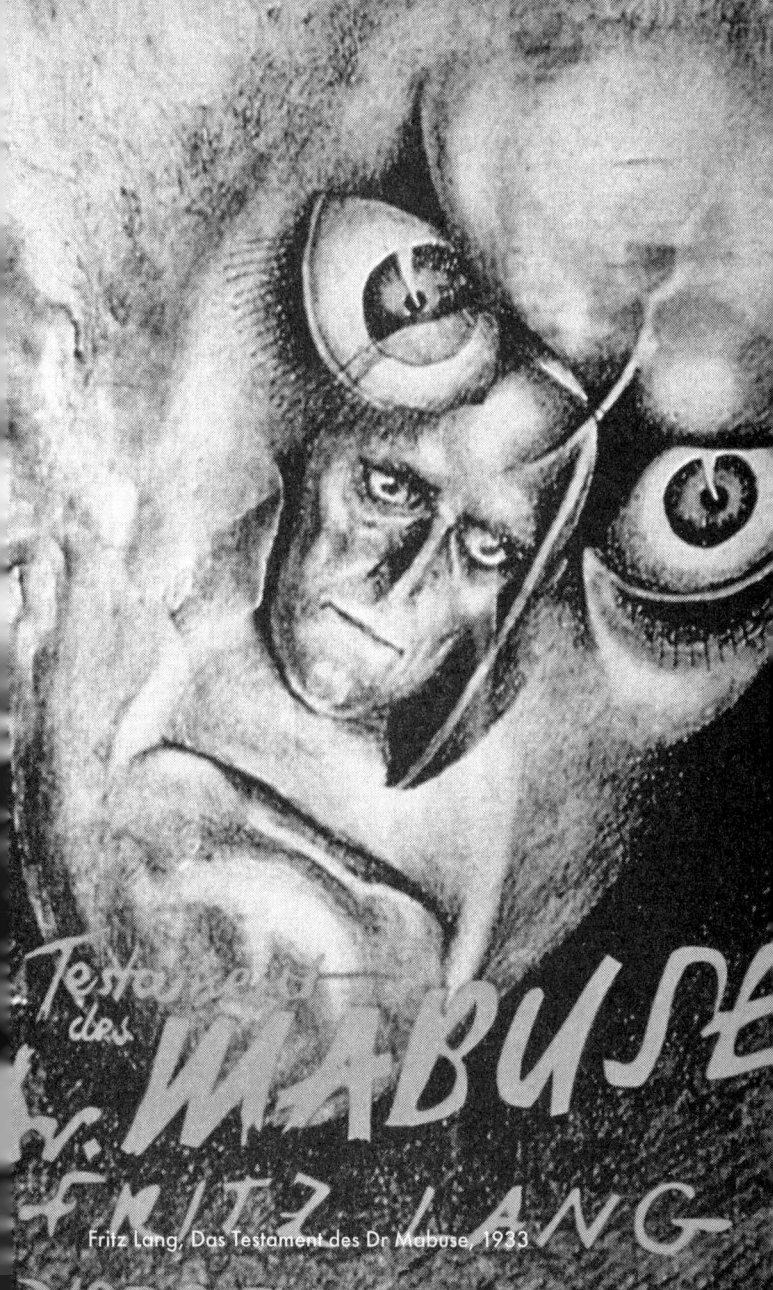

Fritz Lang, Das Testament des Dr Mabuse, 1933

Philippe Halsman, Salvador Dalí with Magnifying Glass, 1946

to blind his facade by rendering it opalescent – or, more accurately, glassy, as we say of diseased eyes – with the glass remaining transparent only in the undisputed portions of the facade. Could it be that architecture, as an art of vision and artifice, is like Argus Panoptes, the hundred-eyed watchman of Greek mythology who could guard and sleep simultaneously, closing half his eyes while keeping the other half open?[107]

But the gaze is also that of the camera, whose glass eye captures the world, enchants it and eroticises it, just as Werlemann does when he translates the fictional potential of the villa into images. And more than architecture, it was cinema – the fantasy technology par excellence, the most popular modern medium and the most machinic visual art – that Dalí sought to conflate with surrealism.

Dziga Vertov, The Man with a Movie Camera, 1929

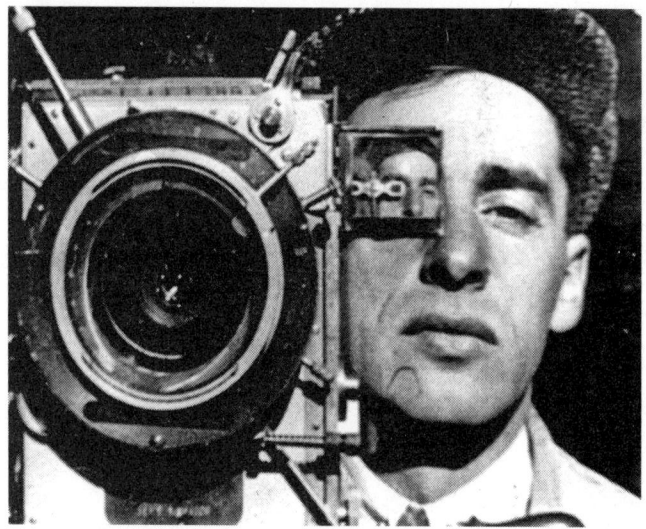

Alfred Hitchcock, Rear Window, 1954

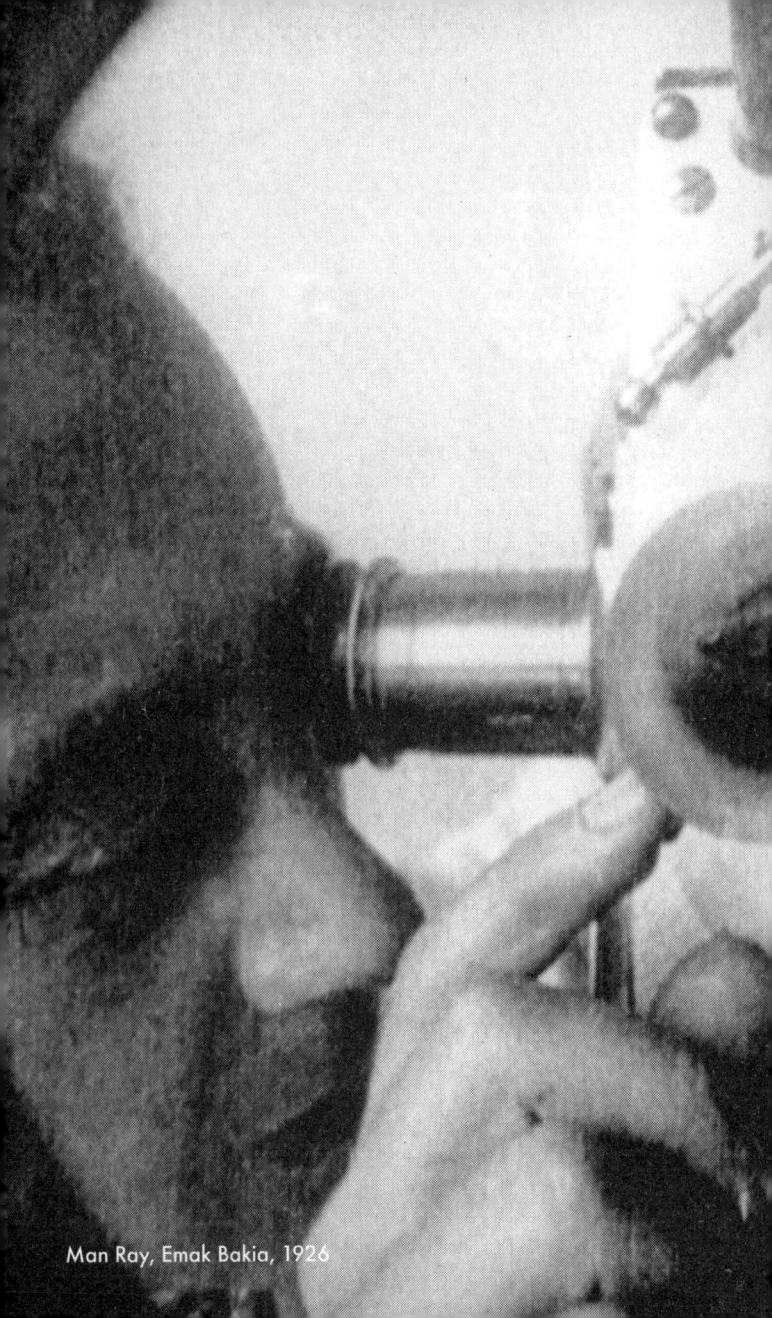

Man Ray, Emak Bakia, 1926

Otto Umbehr (Umbo), self-portrait, 1952

In 1937 he declared in *Harper's Bazaar*: 'Nothing seems to me more suited to be devoured by the surrealist fire than those mysterious strips of "hallucinatory celluloid" turned out so unconsciously in Hollywood, and in which we have already seen appear, stupefied, so many images of authentic delirium, chance and dream… I am just back from Hollywood, and there I heard the word surrealism in every mouth. They have even officially announced surrealistic passages in forthcoming films. This only goes to prove that Hollywood has suddenly discovered all that it has always dimly desired in the subconscious… Reduced to idiocy by the material progress of mechanical civilisation, the public and the masses demand urgently the illogical and tumultuous images of their own desires and their own dreams.'[108] For Dalí, surrealism was the retroactive manifesto of cinema.

The surrealists considered the 'seventh art' of film to be one of their three major activities, along with

Jean-Luc Godard, Le Mépris, 1963

Luis Buñuel & Salvador Dalí, L'Age d'or, 1930

literature and painting. Of the three, according to Breton, it was film that was best suited to 'promoting *real life*'.[109] But no surrealist was more engaged with cinema than Dalí, with some 20 projects over a period of 50 years. Dalí designed sets for Buñuel (the giraffe appears for the first time in *L'Age d'or*, 1930), wrote screenplays (notably, *The Surrealist Mysteries of New York*, 1935) and collaborated with many of the greatest figures in Hollywood. He planned to shoot a film with the Marx Brothers, whom he adored. The project never materialised, though some preparatory designs for the sets survive: one shows a formal dinner on a terrace lit by giraffes transformed into candelabras.[110] For the comedy *The Father of the Bride* (Vincente Minnelli, 1950), he created an anxiety dream sequence that

Vincente Minelli, The Father of the Bride, 1950

Alfred Hitchcock & Salvador Dalí discussing Spellbound, 1944

superimposed a close-up of Spencer Tracy's terrified eyes onto a church aisle. For an animated short film for Walt Disney (*Destino*, 1945), he invented a crossfade technique that allowed for a continuous metamorphosis of one image into another: the translation into celluloid of one of the graphic fantasies of Grandville, whose imagination Dalí drew heavily on, and almost a redefinition in animated form of his paranoid-critical paintings.

However, Dalí's most fruitful collaboration was with Alfred Hitchcock. Many of the English director's chosen themes intersect with those of the surrealists: voyeurism, black humour, extreme experiences such as vertigo, anxiety, psychosis, the impenetrable world of animals... In 1944, Hitchcock asked Dalí, then at the height of his New World fame, to create the dream sequence in what would become *Spellbound*, the screen adaptation of Francis Beeding's *The House of Dr Edwardes* and the first Hollywood film to take psychoanalysis as its theme.[111]

'I requested Dalí because of the architectural sharpness of his work. Chirico has the same quality, you know', said Hitchcock, who wanted a set with 'a very hard image', a hallucinatory precision: 'This was again the avoidance of the cliché. All dreams in movies are blurred – it isn't true!'[112] *Spellbound* is set in a mental asylum that has the ambiance of a family home (which, as the title of the book suggests, could equally well be the house of Dr Blanche, who tended, in his asylum in Saint-Cloud, to the needs of a whole generation of romantic artists tormented by spleen and hereditary conditions). The plot revolves around the double resolution, through psychoanalysis, of a crime and a mental disorder. The denouement sees the patient cured of amnesia and the identity of the murderer revealed – to be none other than the director of the asylum. This theme, along with the film's final scene, flags the influence on Hitchcock of *The Cabinet of Dr Caligari* (Robert Wiene, 1920), a film that so fascinated the partners of OMA that they initially wanted to name their office after it.[113] The first masterpiece of German

Salvador Dalí on the set of Spellbound, 1944

French poster for Alfred Hitchcock, La Maison du Docteur Edwardes (aka Spellbound), 1945

expressionist cinema, Wiene's film astonished contemporary audiences with its sets – painted canvases that were conceived as integral to the story. This was probably the reference Hitchcock had in mind when he hired Dalí, even if he sweetens Wiene's intentions to suit the tastes of Hollywood and gives the film a rather syrupy happy ending. And the same goes for Dalí, who visibly attempts to reconnect with the avant-garde with his scenario for the dream/nightmare sequence related by the patient – a fiction within a fiction and the pivotal moment that tips the plot of the film towards its denouement.

The large painted decorations that Dalí designed for the set assemble three of the commonplaces of modern architecture – a 'curtain' wall, a flat roof and a ramp – in order to turn them into agents of anxiety and vertigo.[114] A man falls like a stone from the roof. The patient runs down a tilted plane, trying to escape a terrifying flying shadow. A man armed with giant scissors cuts, one by one, the open eyes that cover a curtain, revealing another cloth underneath, then another: Dalí

Salvador Dalí, study for the dream sequence of Spellbound, 1944

Alfred Hitchcock, Spellbound, 1944

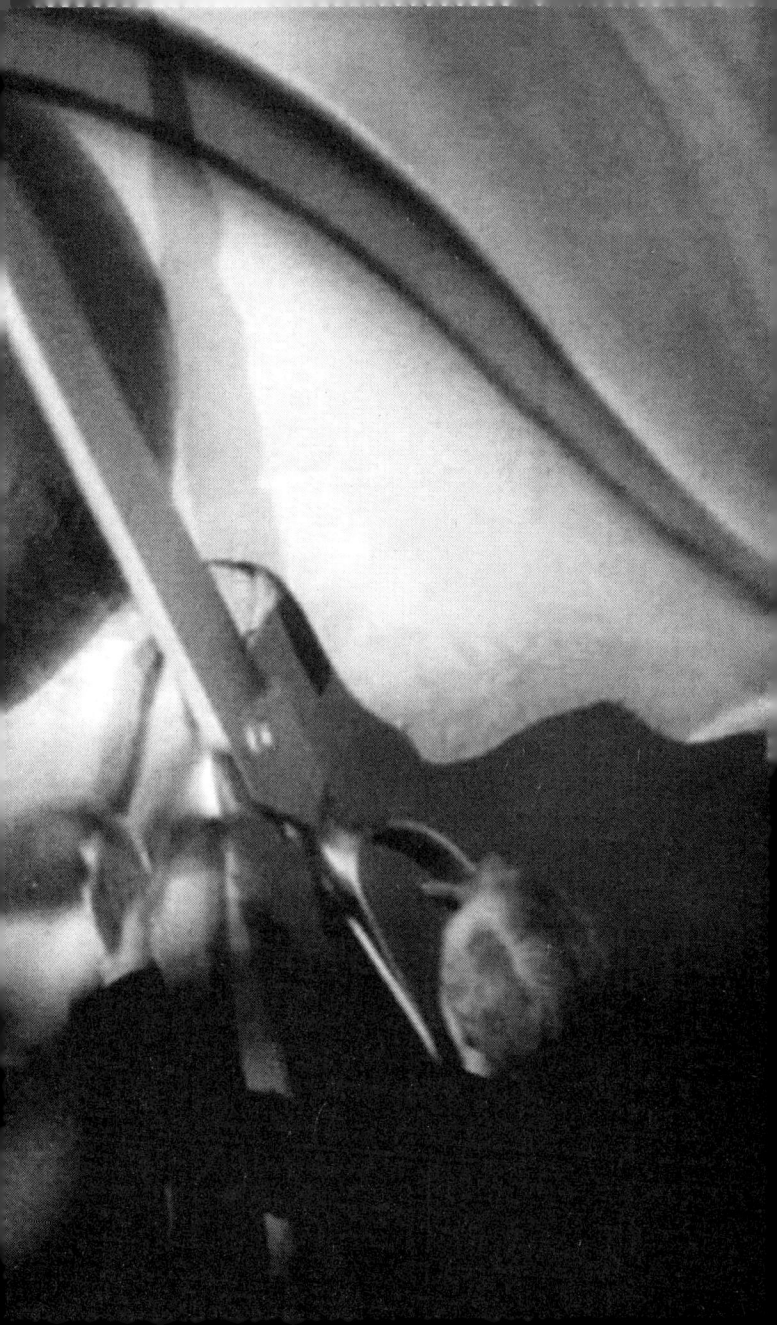

fuses the inventions of Wiene and Buñuel into a parable of blinding. However, these eyes which no longer see will recover their powers. The psychoanalytic interpretation of the dream will prove that the ramp was the cause of a tragic accident in the patient's childhood, the memory of which he had repressed, giving rise to his guilt and amnesia. Re-enacting the scene in reality, the patient is freed from his psychosis.

The Dalínian episode in *Spellbound* could be the stuff of one of those fables that OMA were so fond of around the time of *Delirious New York* that they presented several of them as 'fictional projects' to conclude the book. These would tell of how the amnesia of modernity would be cured, thanks to a dream, paving the way for its resurrection through a project of 'hallucinatory precision' – the Villa dall'Ava. The emblematic architectural moments of this project – the facade that is free but blind, the ramp

Alfred Hitchcock, Spellbound, 1944

descending towards the metropolis and the vertiginous roof terrace – would then be recomposed by the camera and diffused via the freeze-frames of *S,M,L,XL*.

A living set, a modernist parody, a Dalínian joke, a fictional object – the villa is all of these things at once. As such, it is designed as a concrete demonstration of the second modernism advocated by OMA, which seeks to give new life to the first one by infusing it with the most radical avant-garde of all – surrealism. Here, Koolhaas is testing the feasibility of this architecture with a programme that is both routine and potentially heroic: a villa, the one commission for which the client is singular enough, and strong enough, to demand a masterpiece from the architect[115] – and to accept the consequences. In doing so, he replays what Le Corbusier did in his own time, not so far away from here, and defuses the 'intimidation' represented by his nearby purist villas. The Villa dall'Ava thus stands as the prototype for a metropolitan architecture for the present day, where the exhilarating madness of modernity can express itself anew, liberated from the depths in which it had been submerged by the functionalist superego.

But this little construction is also, as I have tried to demonstrate here, a dense compression of cultural references, shaped by the spirit of the avant-garde and subtly irrigated by its author's ties to multiple historical filiations. Whether conscious or not, literal or reinterpreted, these references catalyse the almost chemical reaction that takes place in the conceptual crucible that is the villa. Once again, the tormented quest of mannerism comes to mind. The mannerists, writes historian Patricia Falguières, defined themselves by a triple awareness – of being modern, of coming to the end of an already long and rich history of art, and of inheriting an 'ascendant phase of which Michelangelo constitutes the unsurpassable summit'.[116] (With the added complication that the master himself pointed out the path of deviance, as Koolhaas was able to ascertain in Florence in 2006.[117]) Believing they were living in a kind of end time, these artists laid claim to an art that was, self-consciously, an anticlassicism synonymous with a 'revolt within the very spirit of classicism'.[118] A sixteenth-century avant-garde, paradoxically beset by the melancholic mindset of those who come 'after', mannerism sought to balance a love of the masters with a desire to surpass them. Which gives pause for thought: are the doctrines and works born of periods of historical renewal, from the Renaissance to the modern movement, as much a curse as an opportunity? A journalist once recounted how he had asked Koolhaas – somewhat unwisely – if he knew of Moholy-Nagy's *Light Space Modulator*, thinking he could detect traces of it in the sophisticated luminosity of the side facade of the Villa dall'Ava. "'Unfortunately", Koolhaas replied, with a Mona Lisa smile, "I know everything"'.[119] So, could it be that what this little house reflects is not so much the chaos of the world as its architect's theoretical and material anxieties, his never-ending quest to be avant-garde, *after all*? As the manifesto of a fertile revolt against the limitations of modernism executed in the very spirit of modernism, the Villa dall'Ava crystallises a question that seems more relevant than ever today: how do we continue to invent, knowing full well that everything has already been said?

Rem Koolhaas at the Villa dall'Ava, 1991

THE VILLA OF MYSTERIES

1. From the English version of Antonioni's *Quel Bowling sul Tevere*, translated by William Arrowsmith (New York: Oxford University Press, 1986), 71.
2. Text first published in *Cahiers Renaud-Barrault*, no 59 (1967). English version in Michel Foucault, *Language, Counter-Memory, Practice*, translated by Donald F Bouchard and Sherry Simon (Ithaca: Cornell University Press, 1977).
3. Bernard Leupen and Christoph Grafe, 'Een metropolitane villa: OMA's Villa dall'Ava in Parijs', *Archis*, no 1 (1992); Bart Lootsma, 'Villa dall'Ava, Paris', *Bauwelt* 83, no 9 (1992), 420–31; Jacques Lucan, 'Villa dall'Ava, Paris – Une construction moderne', *Le Moniteur AMC*, no 28 (1992), 26–35/*Domus*, no 736 (1992), 25–35; Jean-Louis Cohen, 'Suburban Subversion', *Progressive Architecture* 73, no 4 (1992), 114–21. The articles have been published in English in 'Villa dall'Ava (1986–1993), A Tiny Bit Perverse', in *OMA/Rem Koolhaas: A Critical Reader from Delirious New York to S,M,L,XL*, edited by Christophe Van Gerrewey (Basel: Birkhäuser, 2019), 246–71.
4. François Chaslin, 'Sous la piscine exactement', *Le Nouvel Observateur*, no 1437 (1992), 178–80, reprinted under the title, 'Déséquilibres – Sous la piscine exactement', in François Chaslin, *Deux conversations avec Rem Koolhaas et caetera* (Paris: Sens & Tonka, 2001), 169–78; Jean-Paul Robert, 'Villa dall'Ava à Saint-Cloud', *L'Architecture d'Aujourd'hui*, no 280 (April 1992), 10–19. English versions in Van Gerrewey, ibid.
5. *La Villa dall'Ava*, directed by Richard Copans, Arte et les Films d'ici, 1995. This 26-minute documentary came out the same year as *S,M,L,XL*.
6. Christophe Van Gerrewey, *Reality Without Restraint: Bathtime in the Villa dall'Ava* (Ghent: Vlees & Beton, 2005).
7. Sigmund Freud, 'The Moses of Michelangelo' (1914), in *The Standard Edition of the Complete Psychological Works of Sigmund Freud*, vol 13, translated and edited by James Strachey (London: Hogarth Press and the Institute of Psycho-Analysis, 1955), 212; translation slightly modified. And Freud goes on: 'To discover his intention, though, I must first find out the meaning and content of what is represented in his work: I must, in other words, be able to interpret it. It is possible, therefore, that a work of art of this kind needs interpretation, and that until I have accomplished this interpretation I cannot come to know why I have been so powerfully affected. I even venture to hope that the effect of the work will undergo no diminution after

8. OMA has built practically nothing in Paris. As of 2024, its list of realised works was limited to the interior design of Le Dauphin restaurant (with Clément Blanchet, 2010) and the refurbishment of an industrial building in the Marais quarter for the Fondation Galeries Lafayette (2012–18). Its only sizeable realised project, LabCity CentraleSupélec (2013–17), is located on the Plateau de Saclay around 20km southwest of Paris.
9. Rem Koolhaas, *Delirious New York: A Retrospective Manifesto for Manhattan* (London: Thames & Hudson, 1978). Page references in this text are to the second edition published by Monacelli Press in 1992.
10. OMA, Rem Koolhaas and Bruce Mau, *S,M,L,XL* (New York: Monacelli Press, 1995).
11. 'I wanted to talk about the villa. "I have an incredible fatigue with describing my own work", the 47-year-old architect said with a sigh of existential impatience, and then, in impeccable French, he ordered the waiter at the Ritz to bring him scrambled eggs and bacon. I persisted. Koolhaas stuck to his silent guns, allowing only that "the reaction to the house has been euphoric", a piece of news that seemed worrisome to him.' See Charles Gandee, 'The Ideal Villa', *House & Garden*, no 3 (1992), 158–72, reproduced in Van Gerrewey, op cit, 254. See also Koolhaas's deflection of François Chaslin's attempts to get him to confirm his critical interpretations in *Deux conversations avec Rem Koolhaas et caetera*.
12. Architect and graphic designer Joseph Cho has produced a subtly illuminating analysis of *S,M,L,XL* that proposes to read the thick volume and the graphic strategies that unfold behind its abstract cover as analogues of Bigness, the 'quality' of the very large-scale buildings theorised in one of the book's main essays (which was itself derived from the analysis of the skyscraper in *Delirious New York* and, more broadly, from the architectural strategies exemplified by the OMA projects presented in *S,M,L,XL*). See Joseph Cho, 'S,M,L,XL, suivez le guide', *Le Visiteur*, no 7 (Fall 2001), 112–33.
13. 'Manhattan is the twentieth century's Rosetta Stone', *Delirious New York*, 9.

FREEZE-FRAMES

14. 'Architecture: Pour qui? Pourquoi?', *L'Architecture d'Aujourd'hui*, no 285 (April 1985), 71.
15. Koolhaas, in a lecture given on 24 September 2015 as part of *ZEROnow: A Symposium on the Topicality of ZERO* at the Stedelijk Museum, Amsterdam.

16. Video available online at https://www.oma.com/lectures/zero.
17. A detail that seems all the more curious given that the letter in question (or at least the one shown in the Copans film *La villa dall'Ava*) was written in black ink.
18. 'Le Corbusier (ground floor), under Mies van der Rohe (rotated main floor) covered by Gehry materials and Tadao Ando sides.' Charles Jencks, 'The Tragedy of Rem Koollhaas', *ANY*, no 9 (1994), 41–45.
19. Mies van der Rohe's Farnsworth House, Philip Johnson's Glass House, Le Corbusier's Villa Savoye. It is not clear, however, whether he is claiming them as references or simply identifying the houses in the black-and-white photographs that the director shows him, since he asserts that 'the architecture of the house owes nothing to that of the 1920s' (Copans, *La villa dall'Ava*, 6'50").
20. These similarities were pointed out by Michael Graves in 'Accept Being Alone', a discussion with Rem Koolhaas at a conference hosted by Stanley Tigerman. Other participants included Thomas Beeby, Peter Eisenman, Frank Gehry, Leon Krier, Rafael Moneo and Susanna Torre. See Stanley Tigerman (ed), *The Chicago Tapes* (New York: Rizzoli, 1987). An extract from this text, which goes back to the time of the conception of the villa, is included in Van Gerrewey, op cit, 249–53.
21. Rem Koolhaas, 'The House That Made Mies', in *S,M,L,XL*, 63.
22. See Giovanni Brino, *Carlo Mollino: Architecture as Autobiography* (London: Thames & Hudson, 2005).
23. These references come from two lectures, one given by Hans Werlemann at the Berlage Institute in Rotterdam on 16 December 2008, the other at an online event organised by *ARCH+* on 2 December 2020. Titled 'Expanded Photography: The Work of Hans Werlemann', the event reunited Werlemann and Claudi Cornaz, who were in conversation with Stephan Trüby and Zsuzsanna Stánitz. Werlemann and Van der Stelt were both members of Utopia, an alternative visual arts cooperative founded in 1978 in the Watertoren in the DWL quarter in Rotterdam. Werlemann and Cornaz were part of OMA in the 1980s with their production company Hectic Pictures.
24. Lecture given by Hans Werlemann at the Berlage Institute, Rotterdam, on 16 December 2008.
25. Bart Lootsma, 'Hans Werlemann', *De Architect-Thema*, no 51 (1993), 22–23. Published in translation in Van Gerrewey, op cit, 202–03.
26. The film got its belated premiere at the 2020 ARCH+ event, 'Expanded Photography: The Work of Hans Werlemann'.

26. Chaslin, *Deux conversations avec Rem Koolhaas et caetera*, 162. The *Monditalia* exhibition that Koolhaas curated for the 2014 Venice Biennale featured some of the most influential exponents of Italian cinema. The list is reproduced in the catalogue of the show, edited by Rem Koolhaas, *Fundamentals – Catalogue* (Venice: Fondazione della Biennale di Venezia, 2014), 358–59. Besides Antonioni, it refers to the films of Visconti, Rossellini, Ferreri, Straub, Huillet and Tarkovsky, as well as Godard's *Le Mépris*. See https://www.oma.com/projects/monditalia for a pictorial summary.

27. The year after this conversation, in his contribution to the *ZEROnow* symposium, Koolhaas referred to his own activities in the 1960s, journalism and cinema, and showed two images from *L'Eclisse*, including that scene with Delon at the Borsa: 'The 1960s were not only hippies, there was also a very elegant, stark, black-and-white, very orchestrated and controlled 1960s, as here in Antonioni.'

28. The *Monditalia* exhibition at the Corderie explored the modern visual and architectural culture of Italy, taking visitors on a journey from the south to the north of the peninsula. In line with this geographical trajectory, one of its sections, dedicated to cinema, showed excerpts from 82 Italian films based on the locations where they were set. See Koolhaas, *Fundamentals – Catalogue*, 360–61.

29. As well as an installation dedicated to the house that the architect Dante Bini designed for Antonioni in Sardinia: Will McLean, *Antonioni's Villa*, with a text by Niklas Maak.

30. Martino Stierli, 'The Architecture of Hedonism: Three Villas on the Island of Capri', in Koolhaas, *Fundamentals – Catalogue*, 372–73.

31. The remark is Terence Riley's: 'the reproduction of Koolhaas's red-Bic pen is so sharp that it seems as if the architect has inscribed each book personally'. This detail leads him to believe that 'part of the real joy of the book is the quality and craft of its production, which Mau supervised at the printer's plant in Italy'. 'Chute libre', *L'Architecture d'Aujourd'hui*, no 304 (April 1996), 57–58.

32. *S,M,L,XL*, 180.

33. Bart Lootsma, 'Now switch off the sound and revert the film: Koolhaas, Constant and Dutch Culture in the 1960s', *Hunch*, no 1 (1999), 152–73.

34. Marida Talamona, *Casa Malaparte* (Milan: Clup, 1990). The original Italian edition went through five reprints and was translated into French and then English. Among other things, the historian demonstrates that Malaparte borrowed his fabled tapering staircase from

the church in Lipari, where he had been exiled by Mussolini in 1934. One of the principal attacks on this book in Italy came from Franco Purini in an article, 'Architettura senza architetto' (Architecture Without an Architect), *Casabella*, no 582 (1991), which attempted to refute Talamona's research and reinstate Libera as author of the villa, denouncing the idea of 'architecture as a derivative of literature'.

WAYWARD SAVOYE

35. Quotes are from the translated and reprinted versions of their articles in Van Gerrewey, op cit, 262 and 231.
36. In his presentation of the Villa Savoye. Le Corbusier and Pierre Jeanneret, *Oeuvre complète*, vol 2, 1929–1934, edited by W Boesiger and O Stonorov (Zurich: Les Éditions d'Architecture, 1964), 24.
37. Le Corbusier and Jeanneret, *Oeuvre complète*, vol 2, 27.
38. In the most in-depth study to date of the Kunsthal in Rotterdam, Tibor Pataky sees the ramp at the Villa dall'Ava as the first instance of OMA's exploration of this Corbusian motif. He also notes how this reference to Le Corbusier is systematically muted by Koolhaas, notably in the 'Ramp' volume of the *Elements of Architecture* series published in 2014 to accompany the Venice Biennale that he curated. See Tibor Bonaventura Pataky, 'Inventory of Problems: The Genesis of the Rotterdam Kunsthal by OMA/Rem Koolhaas, 1987–1992', PhD thesis (EPFL Lausanne, 2021), 254.
39. See Thomas Schumacher, 'Deep Space, Shallow Space', *The Architectural Review*, no 1079 (January 1987), 37–42.
40. *S,M,L,XL*, 181.
41. Le Corbusier and Jeanneret, *Oeuvre complète*, vol 2, 1.
42. Catherine de Smet, *Le Corbusier, un architecte et ses livres* (Baden: Lars Müller, 2005), 7–8.
43. Advertisement for *Vers une architecture* published in *L'Esprit nouveau* in 1924 and 1925. See Smet, *Le Corbusier*, and Beatriz Colomina, *Privacy and Publicity: Modern Architecture as Mass Media* (Cambridge, MA: MIT Press, 1994).
44. Cho goes on: 'Texts and projects are often disrupted by seemingly random moments which break an otherwise continuous train of thought: an advertisement for men's underwear interrupts the presentation of a project for the Frankfurt airport, or suddenly in the middle of the pages devoted to a housing project in Berlin, a photograph of what looks to be a surgical operation on the corpse of Lenin occupies a double-page spread. Multiple, disparate images will often be combined into the presentation of a project

in an apparently haphazard fashion. These momentary interruptions and juxtapositions, organised around a non-linear sequence of chapters, produce an episodic reading… Unlike a book that is conceived linearly, *S,M,L,XL* is assembled as a collection of autonomous parts that produce a whole primarily by virtue of being bound together in one book.' Cho, 'S,M,L,XL, suivez le guide', 128.

45. This Dr Esprit Blanche (1796–1852) happened to be a psychiatrist who ran a mental asylum famously modelled on a family guesthouse, whose inmates/residents included Nerval and Maupassant, among others. See Laure Murat, *La maison du Docteur Blanche* (Paris: Gallimard, 2013).

46. Emmanuel Petit, *Irony, or the Self-critical Opacity of Post-modern Architecture* (New Haven: Yale University Press, 2013), 205.

47. See Rem Koolhaas, 'Less is More: Installation for the 1986 Milan Triennale, Milan, Italy, 1985', in *S,M,L,XL*, 46–61.

48. Beatriz Colomina has identified some of the references present in the installation: Marcel Breuer's bedroom for Erwin Piscator in Berlin (1927), the gymnasium in Walter Gropius's apartment for the Berlin Exhibition (1931), the exercise areas on the terraces of Richard Döcker's building in the Weissenhofsiedlung, the running track installed by Le Corbusier on top of his Immeubles-Villas (1922), Neutra's Lovell House (1929) and even the postwar conversion of Mies's Tugendhat Villa into a children's gymnasium by the Czech communist authorities. 'OMA's manifesto echoes and transforms earlier manifestos. Even the framing of the project echoes Mies's polemical statements in [the magazine] G, by giving equal value to image and text, and by signing the text.' 'Rewrites', in *Manifesto Architecture: The Ghost of Mies* (Berlin: Sternberg Press, 2014), 25–28.

49. OMA, 'La Casa Palestra', *AA Files*, no 13 (Autumn 1986), 8.

50. Roberto Gargiani, *Rem Koolhaas/OMA: The Construction of Merveilles* (Lausanne: EPFL, 2008).

51. Petit, op cit, 183.

52. 'A mannerist collage to take your breath away' is how François Chaslin described the villa in *Deux conversations avec Rem Koolhaas et caetera*.

53. Nikolaus Pevsner, 'The Architecture of Mannerism', in *The Mint*, edited by Geoffrey Grigson (London: Routledge, 1946); Bruno Zevi, 'Introduzione: attualità di Michelangiolo architetto', in *Michelangiolo architetto*, edited by Paolo Portoghesi and Bruno Zevi (Turin: Einaudi, 1964); Manfredo Tafuri, *L'architettura del manierismo* (Rome: Officina, 1966). This

aspect of the historiography of mannerism and the resonances of this 'style' through time have been examined with particular reference to these texts by Andrew Leach in 'The Mannerist Imperative', *Project*, no 4 (2015), 44–49.

54. AMO, Charlie Koolhaas, Rem Koolhaas, Manuel Orazi: 'Biblioteca Laurenziana', *Fundamentals – Catalogue*, 404–05. At the Biennale, the display was placed opposite a Gabriele Mastrigli installation devoted to Superstudio.

55. Critical reaction to the installation was extremely mixed. Some, quite predictably, saw a logical connection between Koolhaas's remarks on the deformation of the fundamentals of architecture and his proposal for the biennale. 'Michelangelo's mannerist manipulation of architectural elements (wall, window, door, stair) directly alludes to Koolhaas's investigations in the Elements of Architecture exhibit in the Central Pavilion' (John Hill, *World Architects*, 11 June 2014). Others found in this unexpected meditation an acid melancholy, 'a kind of scream, an architect looking back to see that architecture was once better, was once part of art, a thing that could scare and thrill just through proportion and a subversion of the basic elements. It is the very last thing you might expect to find here amid the encyclopedic nihilism of this brilliant and frustrating show – nostalgia, not just for the lost modernism on display but also for what came before' (Edwin Heathcote, *FT*, 13 June 2014). The then curator of architecture, design and digital at the V&A in London noted that Koolhaas 'clearly has had some kind of epiphany at the library', but decided this was 'due to the excesses of a particular style and the solution is to limit our contact with it. This is a kind of puritanism, even self-punishment' (Kieran Long, 'Elements Makes You Unutterably Sad for Koolhaas and What He Thinks Architecture Is', *Dezeen*, 12 June 2014).

56. See Irina Davidovici's pioneering study of the historiography of mannerism, its interpretations and manifestations in architecture from the sixteenth century to the present day, 'Abstraction and Artifice', *OASE*, no 65 (2004), 100–41.

57. For the historian Christoph Schnoor, it was indeed Colin Rowe who brought mannerism earlier on into the architectural debate: 'One of the strengths of Colin Rowe's theory is the notion of ambivalence. Rather than seeing it as a weakness of a design or an urban situation, Rowe would formulate the double meaning as a gain, as a successful principle of architectural thinking. Of course, this had to do with his rejection of the modernist idea of straightforward directness and clarity. Thus, he could only be

appalled when he was obliged to accept that a younger architect, Robert Venturi, somehow not only made use of the principle but also made it appear that he had invented it... But it had been Rowe who had first developed this idea of an ambivalent reading of architecture, based on mannerist architecture.' See Christoph Schnoor, 'The Compromised Slab – Koolhaas and Kollhoff Interpreting Colin Rowe', in *Proceedings of the 34th Annual Conference of the Society of Architectural Historians, Australia and New Zealand, 'What Does History Have in Store for Architecture Today?'* edited by Gevork Hartoonian and John Ting (Canberra: Sahanz, 2017), 629–40. https://www.sahanz.net/wp-content/uploads/SAHANZ-Front-Matter-opt.pdf.

58. Koolhaas, 'Accept Being Alone', in Van Gerrewey, op cit, 253.
59. Koolhaas, *Delirious New York*, 10.
60. Colin Rowe's famous essay was first published in *The Architectural Review* in March 1947 and then collected in the anthology, *The Mathematics of the Ideal Villa and Other Essays* (Cambridge, MA: MIT Press, 1982).
61. See his scathing portrait of Rowe in 'La deuxième chance de l'architecture moderne: Entretien avec Patrice Goulet', *L'Architecture d'Aujourd'hui*, no 23 (April 1985), 2–9.

'I remember the first time I saw Colin Rowe: it was in the big room in the basement where he worked. There was a terrible smell, barely any light and an enormous sick dog, its black coat full of red lumps, like Tschumi's project for La Villette. A solitary student, black, worked at a table and, leaning over him, Rowe whispered "Palazzo Pitti, Piazza Navona…" into his ear, as if they were pornographic expressions. It was one of the most shocking scenes I've ever witnessed but it tells you a lot about American architecture. The modernism of Colin Rowe – because in his own way he was one of the harbingers of modernism – was completely amputated from its social programme, the social being for him the height of ridiculousness. In his book, *Collage City*, there's a very revealing phrase, about allowing the city to "enjoy utopian poetics without the need to suffer from utopian politics." It was the first time I'd encountered this typically Anglo-Saxon predisposition, which has since become more and more dominant.' Nevertheless, Schnoor argues that Koolhaas's IBA competition project 'Shipwrecked' in Berlin (1984–87) displays some design moves that are not unlike some ideas advocated by Rowe in *Collage City* (1978), since it uses 'modernist architectural precedents from the vicinity.' Schnoor, *The Compromised Slab*, 633.

FLAGRANT DALÍ

62. Madelon Vriesendorp, *The Arrival of the Floating Pool*, 1975.
63. Richard Ingersoll, 'Rem Koolhaas and Irony', *Casabella*, no 610 (1994), 16–19, reprinted in Van Gerrewey, op cit, 231; Gargiani, *Rem Koolhaas/OMA*, 135–41.
64. *Architecture d'Aujourd'hui*, directed by Pierre Chenal (1930), script by Pierre Chenal and Le Corbusier, http://vimeo.com/67793221.
65. Bruce Chatwin, 'Self-Love among the Ruins', *Vanity Fair*, April 1984, 46–107. About the architecture of the villa, Chatwin adds: 'The walls were the colour of bull's blood, the windows were like the windows of a liner and there was a wedge-shaped ramp of steps which slanted, like a sacred way, up to the terrace roof.'
66. Man Ray, *Self-Portrait* (London: Andre Deutsch, 1963), 226.
67. Marie-Laure de Noailles, a descendant of the Marquis de Sade, financed the purchase and publication of the manuscript of de Sade's *The 120 Days of Sodom*, from which Luis Buñuel would take the character of the Duc de Blangis for the shocking final scene of *L'Age d'or*, also financed by the Noailles. Man Ray was obsessed with de Sade, as evidenced by his many 'homages' – painted, sculpted and photographed – to the Marquis, the most famous being his portrait in profile in front of a burning Bastille, dated 1938.
68. Long before that, a film scripted by Rem Koolhaas and René Daalder, *De Blanke Slavin* (1969), was also set in a sulphurous building that had fascinated Koolhaas since childhood: the Saint Hubertus hunting lodge near Otterlo (1915–20), designed by H P Berlage for the Kröller Müller family (Rem's mother was a friend of Hélène Kröller Müller). This brick mansion with its belltower was conceived as a *Gesamtkunstwerk*, entirely decorated and furnished by the architect and set in a park that he had also landscaped. See Ingo Niermann, 'Interview with Rem Koolhaas', *Fiktion*, 30 September 2016.
69. Rem Koolhaas, 'Delirious New York', *L'Architecture d'Aujourd'hui*, no 186 (1976), 36.
70. In the chapter on 'Caravaggio and Surrealism' in the same volume, written after his return from the United States, Le Corbusier interprets the American taste for surrealism as a sign of decadence, contrasting it with 'cubism, the lucid gesture of constructive spirits seeking the conquest of the new times ... a powerful revolution.' *When the Cathedrals Were White*, 147.
71. 'I have had a long interest in surrealism but more for its analytical powers than for its exploitation of the subconscious or its aesthetics... I was most impressed by its

paranoid methods, which I consider one of the genuine inventions of this century, a rational method which does not pretend to be objective, through which analysis becomes identical to creation.' See Alejandro Zaera Polo, 'Finding Freedoms: Conversation with Rem Koolhaas', in *El Croquis*, nos 53 + 79, 1987–1998: *OMA/Rem Koolhaas*, 33.

72. André Breton, *Qu'est-ce que le Surréalisme?* (1934), quoted by Dawn Ades in *Dalí* (London: Thames & Hudson, 1995), 119.

73. See Shumon Basar and Stephan Trüby (eds), *The World of Madelon Vriesendorp* (London: AA Publications, 2008). The book accompanied a travelling exhibition originating at the AA in January 2008.

74. For an illuminating discussion of this subject see the chapter, 'Position morale du surréalisme', in Astrid Ruff, *Dalí et le dynamisme des formes* (Dijon: Les presses du réel, 2009).

75. Over the course of his life, Le Corbusier amassed a collection of 2,300 postcards which he never spoke about and which remained secreted away in his studio. See Luis Burriel Bielza, *Le Corbusier: La Passion des cartes* (Brussels: Mardaga, 2013).

76. *S,M,L,XL*, 312 and 316. The first entry is taken from Aldous Huxley's *Brave New World* (1932), the second (partly quoted here) comes from Gertrude Jobes, *Dictionary of Mythology, Folklore and Symbols* (New York: Scarecrow Press, 1962). See *S,M,L,XL*, 1288.

77. To these examples we could also add the plans and models of the Très Grande Bibliothèque in Paris (1989), where the reading rooms are likened to big white eggs or the flattened rugby ball of the projection cabin at the Educatorium in Utrecht (1992–95).

78. Johannes Moesman, Pyke Koch and Carel Willink, among others, continued the surrealist tradition in painting. Rem Koolhaas gives some insights into this context in 'Worrying Kindness and Ultimate Wisdom', his conversation with Shumon Basar and Stephan Trüby in *The World of Madelon Vriesendorp*, 258.

79. Rem Koolhaas and Elia Zenghelis with Madelon Vriesendorp and Zoe Zenghelis, 'Sunset at the Allotments', extract from *Exodus, or The Voluntary Prisoners of Architecture* (1972). The project/scenario won a prize in the City as a Meaningful Environment competition organised by the Italian Industrial Design Association and *Casabella*, which used the image on the cover of an issue the following year (no 378, June 1973). The table of contents for the issue was illustrated with a collage on wood by Czech surrealist Jiri Kolàr, *Landscape with Two Lovers*, featuring a giraffe.

80. As confirmed by Elia Zenghelis in a conversation with Cynthia

Davidson in *Log*, no 30 (Winter 2014), 69–105. Zenghelis also recalls the meeting between Koolhaas and Dalí in New York, which was as burlesque as it was disastrous.

81. *Architectural Design*, nos 2–3 (1978), 152–66. The issue also contains a translation, introduced by Dalibor Veseley, of Dalí's text, 'The Terrifying and Edible Beauty of Art Nouveau Architecture' (first published in *Minotaure*, nos 3–4 (1933), with photographs by Brassaï and Man Ray). Surrealism was in the air at the time, with the craze spreading to the general public. That same year, a major exhibition, 'Dada and Surrealism', opened at the Hayward Gallery in London, a curtain-raiser to the triumphant Dalí retrospective hosted by the Pompidou Centre in Paris in 1979–80 – so, two years after its opening – which attracted 840,000 visitors.

AVIDALL'AVA

82. Werlemann, 'Expanded Photography'.
83. One of the rare exceptions is Roberto Gargiani, in the chapter he devotes to the Villa dall'Ava in *Rem Koolhaas/OMA*.
84. Ibid, 141.
85. Some of these animal novellas were translated into German at the end of the 1990s. As far as I know, only two of them exist in English: 'Baldur D Quorg, Spider', in *The Dedalus Book of Dutch Fantasy*, edited and translated by Richard Huijing (Sawtry: Dedalus, 1993), 183–97, and 'Fame, Fortune and the Ant', in *Nice People: A Collection of Dutch Short Stories*, edited by Gerrit Bussink (Montreal: Guernica, 1992), 87–97.
86. Dutch Foundation for Literature, 'Anton Koolhaas: Animal Stories'. http://www.letterenfonds.nl/en/book/830/animal-stories.
87. Bart Lootsma notes that Werlemann's scenario is 'probably a homage to Anton Koolhaas, who became famous for his stories featuring animals. He died when the house was just finished and Rem never wanted the photographs or the film to be used again. This material, which would have loaded the house with references and meaning, has since been forgotten.' See https://ofhouses.com/post/99146790150/105-oma-villa-dallava-paris-france.
88. Werlemann, speaking at the 'Expanded Photography' online event organized by ARCH+ in 2020. The short story by Frans Kellendonk (1951–1990), 'De giraf', appeared in *De kortste verhalen, tweede bundel* (Amsterdam: Tabula, 1986). A French translation, 'La girafe', was published in *Deshima*, no 7 (2013), *Protestantisme en Europe du Nord aux XXe et XXIe siècles*, 267–70.

89. The Loggetta of Cardinal Bibbiena, on the third floor of the Apostolic Palace, was decorated by Giulio Romano (based on a 'pictorial draft' by Raphael) in the 1510s, then rediscovered in 1906 and restored in the 1940s.
90. In Jorge Luis Borges, 'John Wilkins' Analytical Language' (1942), collected in *Selected Nonfictions*, edited and translated by Eliot Weinberger (Viking: New York, 1999).
91. 'The Terrifying and Edible Beauty of Art Nouveau Architecture'. Koolhaas of course borrowed from Dalí's formulation for the title of his essay, 'The Terrifying Beauty of the Twentieth Century'.
92. Gargiani, op cit. On the debt Koolhaas and *S,M,L,XL* owe to surrealism, see also Angelika Schnell, 'Der Berg muss ein Buch werden', *Archplus*, no 175 (December 2005), 78–82.
93. Bart Lootsma also makes the connection between the giraffe and the Eiffel Tower in an article devoted to Werlemann: 'In Werlemann's vision, the giraffe, too, as an endangered species, has found refuge at the home, whilst at the same time its delicate build provides a commentary on the structure of the house itself and its setting: the giraffe is a metaphor of the Eiffel Tower.' Lootsma, 'Hans Werlemann', 22–23.
94. Kellendonk, 'De Giraf'.
95. Davidovici, op cit, 131.
96. Le Corbusier, *When the Cathedrals Were White*, quoted by Koolhaas in *Delirious New York*, 251.
97. See Philippe Duboÿ, *Lequeu: An Architectural Enigma*, preface by Robin Middleton (Cambridge, MA: MIT Press 1986). Duboÿ's book is based on his thesis at the IUAV in Venice, supervised by Manfredo Tafuri, and on numerous articles he published from 1974 on. A revised edition has appeared in French: *Jean-Jacques Lequeu, dessinateur en architecture* (Paris: Gallimard, 2018). When it first came out, the book (a copy of which is still in Madelon Vriesendorp's library in her London flat) met with a mixed reception, alternately admiring, perplexed and even affronted. 'About ten years ago, Duboÿ suggested in an Italian psychoanalytical review that the whole of Lequeu's work and the evidence of his personality ... were fabricated and planted by three different groups of people, though Duchamp was the centre of all three: the first one included Guillaume Apollinaire (who had catalogued the obscene books of the Bibliothèque Nationale), the second one included Georges Bataille, the third, most recent and most brilliant, according to Duboÿ, was a "pataphysical" conspiracy involving Raymond Queneau, Jacques Lacan and the very director of the Cabinet des Estampes, Jean Adhémar

himself... That a plausible case could be put together from the original material, whatever the proportion of genuine to fabricated, is, in itself, fascinating. And it makes Duboÿ's book into a unique document, since in fact the whole text is a punning meditation by Duboÿ on Duchamp, Lequeu and on the joker in the pack – Le Corbusier. From the mid-1920s onwards, Duboÿ would have us believe, Duchamp was meditating a "Showing Up" of Charles-Edouard Jeanneret. He set about this by constructing the anti-figure of Lequeu and slowly feeding him to the outside world. Meanwhile the tissue of puns and association, of *renvois* as Duboÿ puts it ... has become virtually its own independent critico-paranoiac machine and some of the associations are irresistible.

'The drawings in this book are *corpus delicti*, the complete evidence, as presented by Philippe Duboÿ, as the advocate of his true master and accuser in this case, Acteon-Duchamp, against the defender Le Corbusier, Charles-Edouard Jeanneret, whose crime was to misjudge and ultimately to "misplace" the artist in industrial society by an excess of creative vigour. The drawings are therefore the negative counterpart, the black-mirror image of the six volumes which make up Corbusier's *Oeuvres Complètes*. Whether one accepts the charge or denies it, this is how it is set out here. In spite of the inelegance of the presentation, we now have the whole body of the drawings, excellently reproduced. It makes as definitive study of Lequeu as we shall have for some time. The enigma of the title remains unresolved. And that is – perhaps – as it should be.' Joseph Rykwert, 'Pinnacles of Absurdity', *TLS*, no 4369 (26 December 1986), 1439.

98. Emil Kaufmann, *Three Revolutionary Architects: Boullée, Ledoux, Lequeu* (Philadelphia: American Philosophical Society, 1952). Kaufmann believed he could detect a 'certain mental instability' in Lequeu's drawings.

99. Vidler continues, 'He subjected classicism, traditional iconography, institutional programmes, religions, exotic styles, Freemasonic practices and individuals to this relentless play, which took the form of a kind of architectural dismemberment, a physiognomy *en abyme*, which mocked all the verities of the theory of character even as it established, however unwittingly, the subversive codes of a libertine architecture.' Vidler draws a parallel between the mimetic permutations of Lequeu's architecture and the picture-language that Roland Barthes attributed to Arcimboldo in his 1978 essay on the painter. See 'Asylums of Libertinage: de Sade, Fourier, Lequeu', in *The Writing of the Walls: Architectural Theory*

in the Late Enlightenment (Princeton: Princeton Architectural Press, 1987).

EYES WIDE SHUT

100. According to Federica Rovati, Mollino had seen this work by Dalí displayed at the Galerie et Colle while on a trip to Paris to see the 1937 World's Fair. See her essay, 'La camera incantata: Carlo Mollino e la scena artistica torinese, 1935–41', in *Carlo Mollino architetto* (Milan: Electa, 2006).

101. See Juhani Pallasmaa, 'Oculocentrism and the Violation of the Eye', in *The Eyes of the Skin: Architecture and the Senses* (1996), which criticises, from a phenomenological perspective, the dominance of vision over the other senses in architecture.

102. *S,M,L,XL*, 233 and 235. Bentham referred to the central observation tower of his Panopticon as 'the Eye of Providence'. OMA's proposal for Arnhem's prison literally splits open the building with two perpendicular axes.

103. Le Corbusier, *Toward an Architecture* (1923), chapter 4.

104. *S,M,L,XL*, 402.

105. *S,M,L,XL*, 442.

106. This image acquires an added piquancy by virtue of the fact that it is said to have been appropriated from an advertising poster for the Amsterdam duty-free shop ('Eye-catching Economy – Amsterdam Airport Shopping Centre'), as shown in the catalogue for the 1979–80 exhibition at the Pompidou Centre, where it is reproduced on page 296. Dalí continued to use this motif well into the 1980s, producing a bronze version called *The Surrealist Eyes*.

107. Son of Gaia, Argus Panoptes would eventually be killed by Hermes, but in grateful memory of his services, Zeus's wife Hera placed his 100 eyes on the feathers of the peacock, her sacred bird. The eye-studded body of Argus and his animal avatar naturally fascinated the surrealists, among them Dalí (*Argus, the Peacock*, 1963); indeed, Argus has had a bewitching effect on the arts, being depicted everywhere from ancient Greek vases to comic strips. A variety of eye-spot butterfly named after him (Argus) appears on the cover of one of Anton Koolhaas's collections of animal short stories, *Weg met de vlinders en anderen dierenverhalen*, 1961. Our iconographic chains and our bestiary are thus enriched by an additional motif.

108. Salvador Dalí, 'Surrealism in Hollywood', *Harper's Bazaar*, June 1937, 68; reprinted in Matthew Gale (ed), *Dalí and Film* (London: Tate Publishing, 2007).

109. Italics in the original. André Breton, *Second Manifesto of Surrealism* (Paris: Gallimard, 1930), and 'Comme dans un bois', *L'Age du cinema*, nos 4–5 (1951).

110. The Marx Brothers film, which envisioned giraffes stuffed with dynamite exploding in Manhattan, was to be titled *Giraffes on Horseback Salad* (1937). See Gale, op cit, and also Luis Buñuel, 'Une girafe', *Le Surréalisme au service de la révolution*, no 6 (May 1933), 34–36.
111. As Dawn Ades points out in *Dalí*, chapter 7, 'Dalí and the Cinema', 203.
112. Interview with François Truffaut recorded in 1962. The full 12 hours of the interview are available online at http://www.openculture.com/2012/02/truffauts_big_interview_with_hitchcock_12_hours_of_free_mp3s.html.
113. See Cynthia Davidson, 'A Conversation with Elia Zenghelis', *Log*, no 30 (Winter 2014), 84.
114. The elaborate dream scene was cut partly for technical and financial reasons, but also because of Hollywood's habit of building certain sets at a reduced rather than 1:1 scale. See Ades, op cit, 204.
115. In his prologue to the presentation of the villa, Koolhaas lists this demand ('The clients wanted a masterpiece') under 'Intimidations II', the first 'Intimidation' being 'Two of Le Corbusier's villas are nearby'. *S,M,L,XL*, 134.
116. Patricia Falguières, in her brilliant work of synthesis, *Le Maniérisme: Une avant-garde au XVIe siècle* (Paris: Gallimard, 2004).
117. Koolhaas, 'Biblioteca Laurenziana': 'By far the most disturbing space I experienced on this journey was the vestibule of the Laurentian Library... Can you compare the violence of the artist Michelangelo's intervention in architecture with some of contemporary artists' more timid involvements in the discipline?... For contemporary artists and architects, the lesson of the Laurentian Library is perhaps that mannerism is a dish best eaten cold and in small doses.'
118. Ibid.
119. Charles Gandee, 'The Ideal Villa', *House & Garden*, no 3 (1992), 158–72.

Salvador Dalí, Rhapsodie modern (Les sept arts), 1957

ACKNOWLEDGEMENTS

This text has gone through several versions, one might even say several incarnations, being reworked and fleshed out without deviating from its plot, the framework of its argument or its structure. It was originally conceived, in a relatively short form, for the catalogue of the exhibition *Oeuvres construites 1948–2009: Architectures de collection Paris Ile-de-France* (Paris: Pavillon de l'Arsenal/Centre Pompidou, 2009), edited by Olivier Cinqualbre and Alexandre Labasse. I would like to take this opportunity to thank Alexandre Labasse for insisting that I accept the commission, despite my initial reservations – I had feared it would be too difficult to go beyond a mere compilation of facts and familiar interpretations in the space allocated – as well as Dominique and Lydie Boudet, who met my flights of fancy with great kindness and elegance.

The initial catalogue entry turned into a lecture, a format more conducive to adaptations, evolutions and improvisations. Various versions of it were given from 2010 onwards in different settings, with its series of accompanying images and associated digressions expanding with each new presentation. I would like to thank my colleagues and friends who have accepted to host its somewhat acrobatic demonstration in their research seminars and lecture series.

These often-elastic oral versions then stabilised into an essay, 'The House of Doctor Koolhaas', published with abundant illustrations in *AA Files*, no 68 (Summer

2014). This time I owe thanks to the journal's editor, Thomas Weaver, whose unfailing trust and support were critical for the delivery of this piece, and to Pamela Johnston for her brilliant translation into English of my French original. A shorter version of this text appeared in Italian in *Casabella*, no 905 (January 2020). Here I want to thank Francesco Dal Co for his interest in my hypotheses, and his astute additions to the iconography, a precious incentive to pursue my investigations.

This particular book – the first of the *Gumshoe* series of architectural mysteries developed alongside Thomas Weaver – therefore constitutes a fourth, revised and much expanded version. It has been facilitated, once again, by Thomas's editorial patronage, and Pamela Johnston's translation and editing. My gratitude also goes to Mari Lending, Christoph Grafe, Tao Zhu and Christophe Van Gerrewey for endorsing both this book and the series as a whole, as well as to Emma Brown for her invaluable assistance in picture research, and Madelon Vriesendorp, Charlie Koolhaas, Hans Werlemann and Teri Wehn Damisch for their generous iconographic loans. Last but not least, this book owes a huge debt to John Morgan, Adrien Vasquez and Teresa Lima, whose compelling graphic design has contributed to enrich my narrative, and to Claudia Caranfa's spot-on cover illustration for this volume – a conclusion to the plot set in motion more than ten years ago by an epiphany one July evening, watching a silent firework display from the heights of Saint-Cloud.

IMAGE CREDITS 4–5 © Hans Werlemann; 11–12 © Madelon Vriesendorp & OMA; 15–22, 25 © Hans Werlemann; 26 S,M,L,XL, 010 Publishers, 1995/photo Nasrin Seraji; 32–35 S,M,L,XL, 010 Publishers; 36, 39–40, 42 © Hans Werlemann; 43 VTR/Alamy Stock Photo; 44 © Christie's Images/Bridgeman Images; 45 © Hans Werlemann; 46 Prismatic Pictures/Bridgeman Images; 47 © Hans Werlemann; S,M,L,XL, 010 Publishers, 1995; 48–49 Michelangelo Antonioni, *L'Eclisse*, 1962; 50–51 Jacques Tati, *Mon Oncle*, 1958; 52 © Hans Werlemann; 53 Frank Perry, *The Swimmer*, 1968; posterspy.com; 54 Billy Wilder, *Sunset Boulevard*, 1950; Michelangelo Antonioni, *La Notte*, 1961; 55 Billy Wilder, *Sunset Boulevard*, 1950; Jacques Tourneur, *Cat People*, 1942; 56–57 Jerzy Skolimowski, *Deep End*, 1970; 58–59 © The Estate of André Kertész/courtesy Stephen Bulger Gallery; 60 © David Hockney/photo Art Gallery of New South Wales/Jenni Carter; 61 bpk Bildagentur/Stadel Museum/Art Resource, NY; 62 © Ed Ruscha/courtesy of the artist and Gagosian; 63 Jean-Luc Godard, *Le Mépris*, 1963; 64–65, 67 S,M,L,XL, 010 Publishers, 1995; 70 © S,M,L,XL, 010 Publishers, 1995; 72 © Fondation Le Corbusier; 73 © Hans Werlemann; 74 © Fondation Le Corbusier; 75 © Hans Werlemann; 76 © Fondation Le Corbusier; 77 © Hans Werlemann; © OMA; 79 © Hans Werlemann; 87 © Charlie Koolhaas; 90–91 Peter Aaron/OTTO, 92 Fundació Gala-Salvador Dalí; 93 Pierre Chenal, *Architecture d'Aujourdhui*, 1930; 94 © Hans Werlemann; 95 NYC Parks' Archived Collection; 96 © Madelon Vriesendorp; 88–101 Man Ray, *Les Mystères du château du Dé*, 1929; 102 PictureLux/ The Hollywood Archive/Alamy Stock Photo; 103 © Madelon Vriesendorp; 104–05 Photo 12/Alamy Stock Photo; 106 Nadezda Murmakova/Alamy Stock Photo; 107 © Madelon Vriesendorp; Koolhaas/ Vriesendorp postcard collection; 108 © OMA; 110 Musée d'Orsay, Paris; © OMA; 111 Album/Alamy Stock Photo; Fundació Gala-Salvador Dalí; 112 © Madelon Vriesendorp; 112 © Charlie Koolhaas; 113 © Philippe Halsman/Magnum Photos; 114 akg-images; 115 © Madelon Vriesendorp & OMA; 116 Digital Image © CNAC/MNAM, Dist RMN-Grand Palais/Art Resource, NY; Metropolitan Museum of Art, Harris Brisbane Dick Fund, 1930, 30.60.1; Archivart/Alamy Stock Photo; 117 Digital Image © CNAC/ MNAM, Dist RMN-Grand Palais/Art Resource, NY; 118 © Madelon Vriesendorp; 119 © Hans Werlemann; 120 Photo © Tate; 121 Bibliothèque de la Ville, La Chaux-de-Fonds; Doisneau/Gamma Rapho; 122–23 *L'Architecture Vivante*, 1929; 124–25 © The Lucian Freud Archive All Rights Reserved 2023/Bridgeman Images; 126–27 © Fondation Le Corbusier; 128–29 © Dominique Boudet; 130 Anton Koolhaas, *De hond in het lege huis*, 1964; Gekke Witte, 1959; *Vleugels voor een Rat*, 1967; *Weg met de vlinders*, 1961; 132–39 © Hans Werlemann; 140 Wikipedia Commons; Bridgeman Images; BTEU/RKMLGE/Alamy Stock Photo; 141 © Museo del Prado; 142–43 © Art Collection 2/Alamy Stock Photo; © Well/BOT/Alamy Stock Photo; 144 Mil image/Alamy Stock Photo; 145 Carel Willink © Sylvia Willink/Pictoright; 146 © Kunsthaus Lempertz/photo Sascha Fuis Photography; 147 Bridgeman Images; 148 Science History Images/Alamy Stock Photo; 150–51 Anonymous, *Paris Métamorphoses*, undated; 152 Bridgeman Images; 153 Güven Güner/Alamy Stock Photo; 154 © Man Ray 2015 Trust/ADAGP – ARS – 2024/Telimage Paris; 155 Charles Cordat, *La Tour Eiffel*, preface by Le Corbusier, 1955; 156 Heritage Image Partnership Ltd/Alamy Stock Photo; 157 © DeA Picture Library/Art Resource, NY; 158 Carlo Bollo/Alamy Stock Photo; 159 © Madelon Vriesendorp; 160 Luis Buñuel & Salvador Dalí, *Un chien andalou*, 1929; 161 Photo Carlo Mollino, courtesy Museo Casa Mollino; 162 Svintage Archive/Alamy Stock Photo; 163 The Picture Art Collection/Alamy Stock Photo; © Madelon Vriesendorp & Teri Wehn Damisch; 164 The New York Public Library/Art Resource, NY; MAXPPP/Alamy Stock Photo; 165 © Christie's Images/Bridgeman Images; 166 Album/ Alamy Stock Photo; Album/Alamy Stock Photo; 167 © Philippe Halsman/Magnum Photos; 168–69 © Fine Art Images/Age Fotostock; 170 © Droits réservés © Musée d'arts de Nantes/photo Cécile Clos; 171 Bischofberger Collection, Männedorf-Zurich, Switzerland; 172 Luc Fournol/Photo12; 173 A Burkatovski/Fine Art Images/Superstock; 174–75 Fritz Lang, *Metropolis*, 1927; 176 Album/ Alamy Stock Photo; Everett Collection Inc; 177 Fritz Lang, *Das Testament des Dr Mabuse*, 1933; 178 © Philippe Halsman/Magnum Photos; 179 Historic Images/Alamy Stock Photo; 180–81 © Screen Prod/Photononstop; 182–83 © Man Ray 2015 Trust/ADAGP–ARS–2024/Telimage Paris; 184 bpk Bildagentur/Sprengel Museum, Hanover/Art Resource, NY; 185 Jean-Luc Godard, *Le Mépris*, 1963; 186–87 Luis Buñuel & Salvador Dalí, *L'Age d'or*, 1930; 188–89 Vincente Minelli, *The Father of the Bride*, 1950; 190 PhotoQuest/Getty Images; 191 Selznick International Pictures/RGR Collection/Alamy Stock Photo; 192 Photo 12/Alamy Stock Photo; 193 Fundació Gala-Salvador Dalí; 194–95, 196–97 Alfred Hitchcock, *Spellbound*, 1944; 201–02 © Hans Werlemann; 218–19 Simon C Dickinson Ltd

The House of Dr Koolhaas
Françoise Fromonot

A Gumshoe book

Concept: Françoise Fromonot and Thomas Weaver
Translations and text editing: Pamela Johnston
Proofreading: Colette Forder

Design: John Morgan studio
Cover art: Claudia Caranfa
Printing and binding: Nørhaven, Denmark
Prepress: farbanalyse, Cologne

© 2025 Françoise Fromonot and Park Books AG, Zurich
© for the texts: the author
© for the images: the artists / see image credits

Park Books AG, Niederdorfstrasse 54, 8001 Zurich, Switzerland
www.park-books.com
T +41 44 262 16 62
E info@park-books.com

Product Safety
Responsible person pursuant to EU Regulation 2023/988
(GPSR): GVA Gemeinsame Verlagsauslieferung Göttingen
GmbH & Co KG, Post Box 2021, 37010 Göttingen, Germany
T +49 551 384 200 0
E info@gva-verlage.de

Park Books is supported by the Federal Office of Culture
with a general subsidy for the years 2021–2025.

All rights reserved; no part of this publication may
be reproduced, stored in a retrieval system or transmitted
in any form or by any means, electronic, mechanical,
photocopying, recording or otherwise, without the prior
written consent of the publisher.

ISBN 978-3-03860-407-5

Coming soon!

MYSTERIES OF A COMMUNIST CAVE

Lytle Shaw investigates the headquarters of the French Communist Party, a building designed by Oscar Niemeyer in the 1960s but not realised until the 1980s, and along the way explores the enigmatic relations between the philosophy of structuralist Marxism and what was conceived as an actual Marxist structure.